LIVING ON THE
EDGE OF DESPERATE

Jennifer Mathewson Speer

Living on the Edge of Desperate

Published by Outcome Publishing
8007 18th Avenue West
Bradenton, Florida 34209
www.outcomepublishing.com

Unless otherwise indicated, Bible quotations are taken from The Holy Bible, New American Standard Version. Copyright © 1960, 1962, 1963, 1968, 1971, 1972, 1973, 1975 by The Lockman Foundation.

First Edition

Printed in the United States of America

1. Religion: Spiritual General
2. Self-Help: Spiritual
3. Religion: Christian Life – Personal Growth

Behold, I am going to do something new,
now it will spring up;
Will you not be aware of it?
I will even make a roadway in the wilderness,
Rivers in the desert.
Isaiah 43:19

Dedicated to my friend
who is often my teacher
Mr. Jim Nicely

1 Thessalonians 5:11

CONTENTS

Forward
Allen T. Speer

We only see desperation as a blessing when we recognize that we can gain greater perspective of Christ in the midst of it. On the edge of desperate, we receive abundant love from Him, even while our heads are bowed and tears fall. That is why Jesus says that those who are poor in spirit (desperate) are the real winners.

In his book, *The Ragamuffin Gospel,* Brennan Manning writes, *"...when we accept ownership of our powerlessness and helplessness, when we acknowledge that we are paupers at the door of God's mercy, then God can make something beautiful out of us."*

During one of the most desperate times of my life, God brought the author of this book into my desperation. It was not a coincidence, but it was God's plan to bring two broken and recently widowed people together, with five struggling children in tow.

Those early years were a challenge for all of us. There have been other challenges since, other days when we have lived as a family on the edge of desperate. Through it all, we continue to see the faithfulness of God.

As you read this book, understand that the author, my precious bride, is a rich blessing to me. God has used her to help me process desperate days and rely on Him. I trust her writing will do the same for you as she points you toward truth.

Indeed, no one experiences the reward of desperation until the cry of desperation creates a place of total surrender to Christ. Every person presented in this book is desperate, but when they bring their brokeness to the Lord, each person experiences more than they expect. They experience the reward of God Himself.

So if you feel desperate, rejoice! Your longing is a gift, your inadequacy is a treasure, and your need is a blessing that can draw you into a deeper relationship with God. The Lord has done a good work in Jennifer and me through desperate days. He will do it for you too.

If you are living on the edge of desperate, you are in good company.

LIVING ON THE EDGE OF DESPERATE

Introduction

The streets were dark as my friends Kathy and Carl Most and I walked back to our Air B&B. As we walked, Kathy and I were discussing desperation…the great needs that unexpectedly arise and interrupt our lives. Certainly, as Christians we know to take those needs to the Lord. And certainly, God meets us in our desperation, but rarely if ever is He interested in restoring our lives to what they used to be. Kathy and I agreed: God uses the desperate seasons of life to change us and to reveal Himself to us in fresh ways. Our conversation that night was driven by earlier events in the evening with a young family who had been living in desperation for quite some time.

Carl, Kathy, and I were staying in a small town in an oppressed country, and on this night, we were visiting a young family who had been through a difficult season. In addition to the hardships of everyday living, this young couple had experienced an unraveling of their marriage and ministry. Their family, as well as their hearts, seemed irreparably broken. Yet my friends and I sensed that hope was alive as we shared a meal in the family's home.

Throughout the evening, we all openly conversed and genuinely laughed, sharing a deep sense of Christ-centered community. We heard both the husband and the wife express tearful stories of God's mercy and grace being poured out on them as individuals and as a couple. Undoubtedly, God was doing a redeeming work in that home, but He was not simply repairing things. Instead, He was changing everything, revealing Himself to a young couple in ways they had never experienced. Nothing about their lives would ever be the same.

The hope-filled events of that evening and my subsequent conversation with Kathy reminded me of a message I had written several years earlier entitled *Living on the Edge of Desperate*. I revisited that message and felt led to expand it into a series. Unsurprisingly, there is no shortage of desperate people on the pages of Scripture. My greatest challenge would be narrowing down the list of truly desperate people in the Bible who take their great need to the Lord yet receive from Him unexpected answers and outcomes.

I've had my own seasons of desperation: being a widow with two young sons, getting remarried, blending a family, battling with cancer, and in these later years, praying and watching from the sidelines the struggles of my adult children. Certainly, we have all walked roads we did not design. We have experienced heartaches we could not foresee. Some of us have struggled in the consequences of our own choices. For most of us, life has either plunged us headlong into desperation, or we have lived on the very edge of it, at least for a season. But like my young friends who were overwhelmed by God's redeeming work in their marriage and ministry, God is at work in you and me as well. In fact, He is always at work.

This is not a self-help book nor is it filled with easy theology. Some of these chapters are hard to embrace, especially when our hearts are hurting. We typically want instant answers and immediate relief, but often God has more in mind. He is not simply repairing our lives so we can get back to normal. He is redeeming, buying back and making new

He is changing everything. He is revealing Himself in ways we could have never known or understood apart from the wrestling and, yes, the suffering. He is taking us into the depths of His love, deeper than we ever asked to go.

We don't like being desperate. In fact, we don't even like the thought of living on the edge of it. We prefer ease and comfort and certainly control. But God is interested in so much more. In her book *Secure in the Everlasting Arms*, Elizabeth Elliot writes,

He makes us wait. He keeps us on purpose in the dark. He makes us walk when we would rather run, sit still when we would rather walk, for He has things to do in our souls that we are not interested in.

As you read, I want you to be encouraged as well as challenged. I want you to put away the false notion that God is primarily interested in our happiness, our health, or our earthly prosperity. Make no mistake—He is deeply concerned with every detail of our lives, and He loves us with an incomprehensible love. His ways, however, are not our ways, and His answers are rarely what we expect. But His outcomes…well, they are infinitely greater than we ever imagined.

If you have read my first two books, you already know my story of loss. Please keep in mind, I do not tell my story because it is better or worse than anyone else's. I tell my story simply because it is the only story I have to tell. God graciously allows me to use my own experiences as I write and teach, lending personal insights to His authoritative Word. In this book, you will read illustrations and accounts that have already been presented in *Women of Grace* and *Women of Hope*. Certainly, I don't want to be redundant, but I encourage you to read any repeated information with fresh eyes in a new context.

Finally, read slowly and ponder long the Scripture in this book. Step into the heartaches, the struggles, and the questions of the people presented in these seven chapters. As you read, bring your own needs and the needs of those you love to the throne of grace where you will find mercy and help. Ultimately, my prayer is that you and I will fully trust the heart of God even when we do not understand it… even while we live on the edge of desperate.

1

DESPERATE
For Life

The word *desperate* probably brings to mind a different picture for each of us. Perhaps for some, it brings to mind a tragedy, loss, or disappointment. Maybe there are faces and circumstances attached to the word that elicit strong emotions, hurt feelings, or memories of crushed dreams. For me, I picture *desperate* as a place: a place a lot like the grimy town of Lago in the 1973 movie *High Plains Drifter.* Truly, no one would ever want to live in this awful town, but for those who do, it seems their souls have been mangled by the collective despair of Lago. Clint Eastwood plays the part of an unnamed drifter who rides into Lago with mysterious plans. By the end of the movie, he paints every building red, renames the town HELL, and burns the whole thing down.

Metaphorically, *desperate* looks—and feels—like Lago. We don't want to live in such a soul-wrenching place, but if we must pass through it, may it be quick and may we exit unscathed. In reality, at times we have all lived in the dusty center of desperate, and at other times we have camped somewhere close to the edge of it. Oh, we would rather burn it to the ground and ride off into the sunset, but God in His sovereign design has something eternal to do within us that can only be wrought in this arid place.

For those of you who would prefer defining rather than visualizing the word *desperate*, there are multiple definitions in Webster's Dictionary. For this study, however, let's keep it simple. *Desperate* means *having a great need*.

Scripture is filled with desperate people. God's people, then and now, are not exempt from hardship, yet hope and comfort abound when relationship with God is front and center. That relationship is through Jesus Christ. He is the way to God, the only way. Christ is our hope, and He beckons us to come to Him when we are weary, broken, sinful, and helpless. He does not make empty promises of health, wealth, and happiness. He does, however, promise His presence as He does a transformational work in us and through us—even while we are desperate.

God is always at work. I want you to hang your hat on that simple truth as you read. Not only is He at work in the circumstances of our lives, but He is accomplishing things we could have never imagined. He is causing all things to work together for His glory—things we are not even spiritually astute enough to ask for. Ephesians 3:20-21 puts it this way: *"God can do anything, you know—far more than you could ever imagine or guess, or request in your wildest dreams! He*

*does it not by pushing us around but by working within us,
His Spirit deeply and gently within us"* (Eugene Peterson, *The
Message*).

In recent years, two particular stories in the Bible not only
have captured my attention but also have been the springboard
for this entire book. And while the stories are chronologically
out of order with the rest of the chapters of this book, the
foundational truth for the entire study begins here with these
two familiar and fascinating accounts of desperation. In both
accounts there is a life- and-death need. In both accounts the
needy parties bring their plea for help to Jesus. But in both
accounts, the Lord responds in ways they never asked or
imagined. Before you read another word of my commentary,
read for yourselves these two stories. You will find them in
Luke 8:40-56 and John 11:1-45.

Desperate Does Not Mean Denied (Luke 8:40-42)

Jesus has returned to Galilea and a crowd is waiting
for Him. An eager crowd. A desperate crowd. Among the
desperate is a man named Jairus. He is not only Jewish but
also a synagogue official. While Jesus' teaching has rebuffed
and irritated many Jewish religious leaders, it has stirred the
possibility of hope in this desperate man.

Every Jewish town had a synagogue. It was the center
of activity: a place of teaching, of gathering, of overseeing
disputes, of marrying and burying. Because Jairus is an official
in the synagogue, he is a man of great importance. He has
power, position, and prestige. And yet on this day, none of
those things matter.

This well-educated, respected man lays aside his position because his need outweighs his accomplishments. Jairus has an only child, a twelve-year-old daughter—and she is dying.

Jairus doesn't care what any of the other Jewish officials believe. He isn't listening to the undercurrent of their disgruntled thoughts. He is a desperate father pleading for his daughter's life. This is not a time for calm, collected requesting. Instead, it is an urgent, life-and-death cry for help. Jairus falls on his face, in the dust, at the feet of Jesus. No flowery speech. No traditional greeting. Just raw, emotional begging.

Remarkably, Jairus has a measure of faith, and he is willing to exercise it. While he may not be able to fully reconcile the firsthand accounts of healing that he has heard with the prophecies he has studied, he considers the possibility that Jesus could be the Messiah. Regardless, in his great need, he casts his life in the direction of faith. He believes Jesus can heal his daughter.

And Jesus says yes.

As He went...may seem like an inconsequential phrase to us (8:42), but it is evidence that Jesus sees the faith of Jairus and is responding. Jesus is going to Jairus' house. Oh, can you imagine the relief that floods this desperate daddy? Perhaps his mind is racing with thoughts. "Jesus is on His way to my house. He is going to heal my little girl. Life will be good again. We can go back to things as they were. My wife and I won't be consumed with fear, and worry, and...."

But nothing plays out like Jairus expects.

18

Often, when we are desperate, we take our great need to the Lord. We know it's the right place, the best place, to carry our burdens. But often, we take our game plan as well. With our great need ,we bring the solution as we see it or want it or imagine it. After all, we are exercising faith, and faith pleases God, right? So, shouldn't we bring our expectations too, maybe even "claim" something that we want to see happen?

Several times you will read in this study: *"His ways are not our ways. His thoughts are not our thoughts"* (Isaiah 55:8-9). Rarely, if ever, does God follow our game plan. He doesn't follow Jairus' plan either. Jairus probably expected Jesus to push through the crowd like a doctor running to triage. Instead, Jesus delays.

For six, long, agonizing verses, the account of Jairus and his dying daughter are put on hold while an unnamed woman interrupts. A woman who has been hemorrhaging for twelve years. A woman who would live another day with or without Jesus' intervention. Jesus seems to be in no hurry as He stops to compassionately deal with her.

The relief that Jairus felt just a moment earlier probably turns to panic. What is Jesus thinking? It seems unfathomable that Jesus would care about something less than life threatening when his little girl is gasping for her last breath. Do you feel it? Oh, dear Jesus, hurry. Please! Hurry!

Have you ever felt this way? Have you, in faith, taken your great need to the throne of grace, praying earnestly for God to intervene, but all you hear is silence? Have you ever awakened in the night tearfully asking God to save a child, heal a friend, relieve a stress…and it seems the ceiling is the only thing listening? I've been there, uncertain of God's ways, His thoughts, and His plans. I have wrestled in the silence and cried in the dark, pleading like Jairus, for God to do something. And do it quickly!

For Jairus, healing is so close. Relief for him and healing for his daughter is palpable —and then, it just stops. The delay, however, doesn't mean that Jesus has forgotten about Jairus or his little girl. *The delay is not a denial of Jairus' request.* Jesus wants to do more than Jairus has ever imagined, even if the delay is momentarily painful.

Dear reader, the Lord hears your prayers. He knows every need you have. But when it feels like heaven is silent, it is good to remember a few things about God. The psalmist writes, *"O my God, my soul is in despair within me; therefore, I remember Thee..."* (Psalm 42:6).

Remember, God is always at work. I have written this twice already. It bears repeating often because we are easily discouraged when we are desperate. God is at work in the circumstances of our lives. Nothing takes Him by surprise. He is not putting us on hold so He can formulate a plan to offset the sudden despair we find ourselves in. He is already at work!

The Old Testament story of Joseph is a perfect example of God at work even when desperate days come calling. Joseph begins life as the favored son of his father, Jacob. Unfortunately, favoritism breeds jealousy and resentment in the other ten brothers. Three times in Genesis 37 the Bible says his brothers hated him. Their hate overflows into a murderous plan to get rid of Joseph. They decide to throw him into a wilderness pit without water and evidently let nature take its course. While Joseph is in the pit, however, the plans change, and he is sold to a caravan of slave traders going to Egypt. The brothers devise a cover story telling Jacob his beloved son has been killed by wild animals (Genesis 17).

Imagine seventeen-year-old Joseph screaming his lungs out, first in the pit and then again as slave traders haul him away. Crying for his brothers to rethink their vindictive plan. Crying for God to rescue him. Silence seems to be the only reply from both family and God.

In Egypt, Joseph is sold to a man named Potiphar, the captain of Pharaoh's bodyguards. In the terrifying circumstances surrounding young Joseph, the writer of Genesis inserts the phrase, *"The Lord was with Joseph"* (Genesis 39:2). In family betrayal, in human trafficking, in humiliating slavery...*the Lord was with Joseph.* In fact, God causes everything under Joseph's care to prosper. God even causes Potiphar and everything in his household to be blessed (Genesis 39:3-5). If we stop reading right there, we could conclude that life is looking up for young Joseph, and that God is coming through in a big way. Sadly, there is no immediate upward trajectory for Joseph. Instead, he is falsely accused by Potiphar's wife of sexual misconduct, falsely arrested, and falsely thrown into prison. Prison in those days was not a place to await a fair trial. Prison was a place to die.

But...*the Lord was with Joseph.*

Even after the latest string of tragedies, Scripture lets us know that the Lord is at work in the circumstances of Joseph's life (Genesis 39:21-23). Joseph's life is not in the hands of any human—not his brothers or slave traders or Potiphar or even Potiphar's wife. His life and his future are decisively in God's hands.

The Hebrew phrase *the Lord was with Joseph* is interesting. It means that God is actively at work. He is not silently standing by watching events unfold. He is not simply riding along. He is not making up a plan as He goes. He is at work, accomplishing His purpose not only in the life of Joseph but also in the life of Joseph's family…and even in the nation of Egypt. Certainly, there must be moments of discouragement when Joseph questions God's ways and plans, when it feels like God is silent or distant or idle. Like Joseph, we must remember that God is always at work, even if we cannot see it or feel it and even if momentarily we don't believe it.

Remember, God works according to His sovereign timing. God is never late and rarely early… this is a painful reality. We like instant answers and quick solutions. Eternal results, however, are rarely instantaneous. God's plans often unfold slowly as He works toward His desired outcome. Like Jairus, we believe God can accomplish anything, but we often wring our hands with anxiety when there seems to be a pause in the action.

A dear Cuban pastor once said, "It takes God a long time to form a heart." Abraham and Sarah are powerful examples of God patiently forming hearts while also working according to His sovereign plans. Genesis 12-21 recounts the tension that is commonly present between God's promises and God's timing.

Abraham is seventy-five years old when God calls him to leave his home and go to a land that God has promised to give Abraham and his descendants (Genesis 12:1-7). Abraham believes God and obeys. He brings along his wife Sarah who is sixty-five years old, beautiful, and hopelessly barren. Neither Abraham nor Sarah understands how God will keep His promise for descendants, but they trust God enough to follow Him.

Years pass. No child blesses the home of Abraham. Tension builds as Abraham suggests a solution for God's seeming delay

(Genesis 15:1-6). God gives Abraham reassurance, but no immediate solution for the dilemma of childlessness. Genesis 15:6 is noteworthy, *"Then he (Abraham) believed in the Lord; and He reckoned it to him as righteousness."* Abraham trusted God enough to settle into the tension between God's promise and God's timing. Sarah, however, has a completely different response.

Sarah carries a burden that does not belong to her. In her aching, childless, impatient heart, Sarah refuses to live in the tension between God's promise and God's timing. She believes it is her responsibility to come through for God and push things along, helping God bring His own promise to fruition. As a result, Hagar, Sarah's slave, is given to Abraham to produce a child in Sarah's place (Genesis 16). The ancient custom sounds reasonable to Sarah. But instead of blessing, the plan produces chaos, strife, and jealousy.

Sovereign God Almighty is undeterred. Even in the wait, even in Abraham's short-sighted suggestion, and even in Sarah's ill-fated debacle, God's plan is unfolding in God's way and, most definitely, in God's time. In Genesis 18, more than twenty years have passed when God reiterates His promise of a child with specifics. *"Is anything too difficult for the Lord?* ***At the appointed time*** *I will return to you, at this time next year, and Sarah shall have a son"* (Genesis 18:14).

The phrase *at the appointed time* is used again in Genesis 21:2 in reference to the promise of a child. It means at the right time, at the set time, at God's time. Do you see it? God set the time for the conception and birth of the promised child long before He ever spoke a word of promise to Abraham. God made an eternal appointment, and He always keeps His appointments. From the beginning He has so much more in mind than simply blessing Abraham's home with a son. He is working out His eternal plan for the redemption of mankind. But on a very personal level, God is forming the hearts of Abraham and Sarah to fully trust Him, even if it means they must live in an unresolved tension for decades.

Dear reader, if we are going to claim the promises of God, we must also claim the timing of God. Proverbs 3:5 reminds us to trust the Lord with all our heart and don't lean on our own understanding—that includes our understanding of God's timing. If God has said it, God will do it. He is never late. Not for Jairus or Joseph or Abraham and Sarah. He is never late for us either.

Remember, our feelings are valid, but truth must prevail. We have been created with emotions. We are a feeling people, yet in times of great need our feelings can be unreliable. Feelings cannot guide us. In fact, our emotions must always submit to truth. If we lean solely into our feelings when our hearts are broken or when our plans are crushed, we will soon come to the wrong conclusion about God. The uncertainty of our emotions will lead us to believe that God isn't good, that He doesn't care, that He isn't listening…and ultimately, that God doesn't love us.

In 2005, my first husband, Dana, died as a result of a car accident. In an instant, all of life shifted for me and for my two young sons. In the months following the accident, my shock gave way to depression. Certainly, my feelings were valid, even normal for such a tragedy. In the ongoing heartache, many elements of my faith in Christ remained firm. I knew the Lord was sovereign and powerful. I knew my husband's life had always been in the hands of God. But somewhere along the way, I began to doubt that God really loved me.

There are two sisters in Scripture who may have felt like

I felt while in the throes of grief. Remember I said earlier two stories from the Bible spurred this series. The account of Jairus in Luke 8 is the first, and the familiar story of Mary, Martha, and Lazarus from John 11 is the second account.

The first five verses of John 11 set up the entire chapter. Jesus, evidently, has had a long-standing friendship with Mary, Martha, and Lazarus. So, when Lazarus becomes ill, the sisters send for Jesus. They fully expect Jesus to come immediately to their home and heal their brother. The Bible seems to affirm the rationale behind their expectations. *"Now Jesus loved Martha, and her sister, and Lazarus"* (John 11:5).

If all we knew of this story stopped at verse 5, how would you anticipate the outcome? The sisters have sent an urgent request to their dear friend. Jesus acknowledges the request in verse 4. Scripture even accentuates the depth of His relationship with the siblings when it declares His love for them in verse 5.

Based on verse 5, I would fully anticipate the story progressing as the sisters expected! That Jesus would rush to their home, kneel beside sick and dying Lazarus, speak to him or touch him or pray over him or something. But the result would be Lazarus getting up off his sick bed, fully healed and praising the Lord. In fact, afterwards, Lazarus would be the highlight of every gathering as he points to the Messiah and gives firsthand testimony of a miraculous healing. Wow! I would want to be on the front row listening and cheering, hoping someday Jesus would love me that much.

Based on our expectations, isn't this what love should look like?

John 11:6, however, shatters every expectation…certainly Mary's and Martha's, and probably yours and mine. *"…but oddly, when He heard that Lazarus was sick, He stayed on where He was for two more days…"* (John 11:6, *The Message*). What? Jesus' delayed response to an urgent need doesn't align with our idea of love. It does not align with the sisters' idea of love either.

When Jesus finally arrives in Bethany, Lazarus not only has died and already been buried but also, according to Martha, his body stinks (John 11:39). Both Martha and Mary have had four days to ponder and stew over Jesus' delay. Both sisters say the exact same thing to Jesus when He finally arrives. In my imagination, Martha speaks with eyes dry and back stiff while Mary trembles with tears running down her cheeks. *"Lord, if you had been here, my brother would not have died"* (John 11:21 & 32).

The sisters are grieving. Certainly, their pain is real, but in their deep sorrow, they are questioning the love of Jesus. They are judging His care for them by their own expectations and their own definition of love. We often do the same thing in times of great despair. We allow our emotions to guide us. We begin to live by what we feel instead of living in truth. We question God's love for us and respond to Him with a note of accusation—*Lord, if you had….*

The Psalms bring such comfort to us because they are filled with very real, often raw, emotion. Almost every psalm of lament begins with a desperate plea, complaint, or outcry from the psalmist. Many of the lament psalms even contain an emotional accusation or question about the compassion of God. But every psalm of lament has a turning point—a moment of realization when the psalmist makes a conscience decision to focus on truth instead of the circumstances and the painful emotions those circumstances elicit. Psalm 77 is a psalm of lament with a definite turning point.

Will the Lord reject forever? And will He never be favorable again? Has His lovingkindness ceased forever? Has His promise come to an end? Has God forgotten to be gracious? Or has He in anger withdrawn His compassion? (Psalm 77:7-9)

Have you ever felt this way? I have. I am so thankful the pages of Scripture are not whitewashed with perfect people giving perfect responses. I am equally thankful that Scripture does not leave us in despair; rather, it always turns us toward truth. Psalm 77 makes a decisive turn in verse 10 as the writer realizes his grief has caused him to misunderstand the heart of God. As he recalls the Lord's faithful deeds in the past, the psalmist changes his focus…and so must we.

*Then I said, "It is my grief that the right hand of the Most High has changed." **I shall remember** the deeds of the Lord; Surely, I **will remember** Thy wonders of old. I will meditate on all Thy work, and muse on Thy deeds. Thy way, O God is holy: What god is great like our God?* (Psalm 77:10-13)

In times of great need, when God seems distant or perhaps uncaring, we must remember truth. In the months following my husband's accident when I felt that God had forgotten to love me and my children, I had to make a conscience decision to embrace the truth of God's Word and to trust the unchanging faithfulness of God. While my circumstances would never be magically altered, my grieving heart found a place to rest.

Even in the pain, He loves us.

Because of the Lord's great love, we are not consumed, for His compassions never fail. They are new every morning: great is Your faithfulness. (Lamentations 3:22-23, NIV)

Though He brings grief, He will show compassion, so great is His unfailing love. (Lamentations 3:32, NIV)

...the Lord's unfailing love surrounds the man who trusts in Him. (Psalm 32:10b, NIV)

"Though the mountains be shaken, and the hills be removed, yet My unfailing love for you will not be shaken nor My covenant of peace be removed," says the Lord, who has compassion on you. (Isaiah 54:10, NIV)

For I am convinced that neither death, nor life, nor angels, nor principalities, nor things present, nor things to come, nor powers, nor height, nor depth, nor any other created thing shall be able to separate us from the love of God, which is in Christ Jesus our Lord. (Romans 8:38-39, NASV)

Oh, it is so easy to lose sight of God's love when we are overwhelmed by emotion. It's easy to forget the goodness of God underneath the weight of our suffering. But precious one, God has proven His love for us once and for all at Calvary. In our hour of great need, we cannot forget His ultimate sacrifice—the mingling of His sorrow over sin with His love for the sinner. While He is working in every detail of our lives, God's greatest demonstration of love is not in the healing of our sickness, the restoration of our finances, or the relieving of our stress. His greatest demonstration of love is that *while we were still sinners, Christ died for us* (Romans 5:8).

Desperate Develops Our Faith (Luke 8:41 & 49-50)

When we are first introduced to Jairus, we are told he is a synagogue official. He is a man with great influence and one who has studied and prepared for the job he now holds. While he is probably not a Hebrew teacher, his position gives him a certain amount of prestige. Like many of us, his identity is interwoven with his occupation. And yet, Jairus does not tout his accomplishments when he comes to Jesus. Desperation has stripped him bare. All the things that once gave Jairus security and identity dissipate in the anguish of his great need.

Desperation is the great simplifier of life. When we become desperate, the unimportant or superficial things of life become glaringly unimportant. The everyday things that often consume us no longer hold our attention. The allure of things that once captured our time and energy diminishes in the heat of desperation.

Likewise, in times of great need, God will allow our desperation to spotlight the things in our lives which we have come to rely on for security and identity. While health, relationships, jobs, and finances are all important, they can unwittingly take the place of trusting the Lord. God's ways are higher than ours. He wants to get rid of any façade or veneer that we have come to accept as reality. He wants to expose our faith for what it really is. As painful as it might be in the moment, God wants to do a work in us that we never asked for or even imagined.

29

Philippians 1:6 says that the work of salvation in us is begun by God through Christ. Because He started the work, He is faithful to complete the work, to see it through, until we meet Him face to face. His aim is not our sinless perfection. His aim is to mature us in Christ, to make us more like Jesus every single day—to sanctify us. This work of maturing us is a lifelong process.

When we have a great need, we typically want the Lord to alleviate it. But our loving Heavenly Father wants to do far more than change our circumstances. He wants to change us. While we want Him to restore life to the way it was before calamity hit, God wants to redeem our lives and our circumstances. *To redeem* means to buy back and make new. We have been redeemed at salvation: all things are made new (2 Corinthians 5:17). But redemption is an ongoing work. Much of redemption involves developing our faith and deepening our trust in Christ.

Listen carefully. God will allow a church, a ministry, a family, or an individual to experience desperate times so that the unimportant or temporal things of this world take their rightful place. As our hearts refocus, God does the tender, yet magnificent, work of maturing us in Christ. This is a hard truth. One that a broken heart might only see in hindsight. There is rest, however, in knowing He is at work, using anything and everything that comes into our lives—amazingly, even the consequences of sin—to deepen our faith.

Let me be clear, calamity does not hit us so that God can teach us great lessons. We live in a fallen world where hard times come, sickness happens, circumstances change. But nothing comes into the life of a believer until it first goes through the loving hands of God. He is not like an ancient, mythological god: fickle and mischievous, toying with human emotions or circumstances. Neither is He the best version of us that we can imagine. Instead, He is completely holy and just. There is no unrighteousness or injustice or cruelty in Him. He is love, and the object of that great love is His children.

Years ago, my late husband and I were asked to lead music at a retreat in Alabama. The keynote speaker was a woman named Jane Bateman. I had never met her, but I was looking forward to hearing her story. And what a story she had to tell!

Throughout the weekend she relayed the painful events of her life; most of those events related to her son Daniel. At the time, I was a new mom. My infant son was also named Daniel. Every painful word Jane spoke, no matter how much grace, truth, and humor she wrapped it in, disturbed me. My immature faith recoiled at the thought of experiencing anything remotely similar, especially if it related to *my* Daniel. In my youthfulness, I silently prayed that no such heartache would touch my family.

To be sure, Jane's story was tragic, but this delightful woman exuded peace and confidence in the Lord. Her faith was amazing to me, yet not amazing enough to abate my fear of the future or my fear of some tragedy invading my life.

At breakfast, on the last day of the retreat, I sat with Jane. After a few minutes of chit chat, I said something foolish. "Jane, if I have to go through what you have been through to know God like you know God, I don't want to know Him that well."

Jane smiled compassionately (perhaps God did too) knowing that every believer will encounter seasons of desperation. If we live long enough, we will all pass through unwanted and unforeseen difficulties that threaten our security and shake our faith. Scripture assures us of this truth yet also encourages us.

Peace I leave with you; My peace I give to you; not as the world gives, do I give to you. Let not your heart be troubled, nor let it be fearful. (John 14:27)

These things I have spoken to you, that in Me you may have peace. In the world you have tribulation, but take courage; I have overcome the world. (John16:33)

Thankfully, our lives are not complicated with knowledge of the future. We cannot see what lies ahead, but we can be confident that Christ is in us and with us. He is always at work, always bringing us to a place of greater maturity. Because Jesus is the overcomer, the victor, His presence is accompanied by His peace—even in the trials. James 1:2-4 addresses the role of trials in maturing our faith. While Jesus underscores our suffering with peace, the passage from James includes joy.

Consider it all joy, my brethren, when you encounter various trials, knowing that the testing of your faith produces endurance. And let endurance have its perfect result, that you may be perfect and complete, lacking in nothing. (James 1:2-4)

In the original language, each phrase of this passage is packed with meaning. So, let's carefully unpack it, phrase by phrase.

Consider it all joy.... Biblical joy has little to do with happiness. While happiness is primarily centered on outward circumstances, joy is an inner contentment only Christ can give. Joy flourishes as we look beyond the discomfort of the circumstances and trust the loving heart of God. We are to consider even the process and timing of His work as joyful. Typically, we want to press the pause button on joy, at least until we see how it all turns out. Joy, however, is available in the process and the timing, as well as the outcome.

...when you encounter various trials.... Never are we able to plan our desperation. We encounter or fall into it unexpectedly. Sometimes the trials are overwhelming, and sometimes the trials are the everyday annoyances of life. Regardless of the degree or depth of the trial, we are sure to experience a variety of them.

...knowing that the testing of your faith.... When we experience a trial, we can be confident that our faith is being tested. The test, however, is not for God to gain insight into our faith. The test is for us to gain insight into our faith. So many times, we verbally espouse a profound faith, only to see it shake like a flimsy reed when a trial blows through our lives. Trials make us aware of the condition of our faith.

...produces endurance.... The purpose of a trial is to produce something in us that is lacking. To produce literally means to put on display. The work that God is doing in us during a trial is not just for our benefit. Instead, He puts His work on display for others to see and be encouraged. When we walk through difficult circumstances, our children are watching us. Our neighbors are observing us. Our co-workers are examining us. Even though their initial response to our suffering might be similar to my thoughtless quip, "I don't think I want to know Him that well," our lives will be an encouragement to others when their own seasons of difficulty arise because they have seen God do an eternal work in us. He is producing endurance.

Let me be quick to say I am not particularly fond of the word *endurance*. It means *to bear up under*. In James 1:2-4, *endurance* means the Lord is not automatically making our pain go away. He is not immediately changing the circumstances. He is changing us as we remain under the difficult circumstances! Through the power of Christ who lives in us, God is cultivating our ability to trust Him even while we remain in the suffering. But why?

And let endurance have its perfect result, that you may be perfect and complete, lacking in nothing.... God's desired outcome for you and me is a mature, unshakable faith in Christ. Listen carefully. God never minimizes our suffering. He never arbitrarily allows great pain to teach us great lessons. Yet in our trials, He reveals Himself to us in ways we could have never known otherwise. Oh, if only we could sufficiently deepen our faith by simply reading our Bibles enough, serving enough, or attending church enough. While all of these things are beneficial to our faith, the valleys of suffering are where we experience our loving, Heavenly Father most intimately. Whether we are in the depths of desperation or living on the edge of it, we can be assured of His great compassion as He deepens our faith and completes the good work of salvation He started in us.

When my children were very young, our neighbors landscaped a beautiful koi fish pond into their front lawn. The project took weeks, and our neighbors were so proud of the final results.

The small pond had a sturdy plastic liner and a small pump that created a lovely fountain of water. As the fountain of water rose and then fell back into the pond, it delicately cascaded over perfectly placed river rocks. Additional flat river rocks were stacked around the perimeter of the pond to add distinction and beauty. Lily pads floated in the water and yard art tastefully surrounded the little pond. The exotic Japanese koi fish, however, were the crowning beauty for the entire masterpiece.

One afternoon I looked out the window of our home to see my four-year-old son standing beside my neighbor's new pond. I was fairly certain his unsupervised visit to the pond would not end well, so I called him home, trying to divert a catastrophe. Sadly, I was too late.

An hour later my distraught neighbor came to my door demanding I see what my son had done to her pond. Her demeanor assured me this would not be a pleasant experience. Dutifully following my neighbor to her koi fish pond, my heart sank when I saw the damage.

My son had done what most little boys would do with rocks and water. He threw the large flat river rocks into the pond delightfully creating magnificent splashes. As a result, there was no fountain spewing water, no dainty trickle cascading over stair-stepped stones. The lily pads were demolished, the yard art overturned…and no koi fish in sight.

"We can't find the koi fish," said my teary-eyed neighbor. Then she added, "Koi fish are prone to heart attacks in stressful situations." I almost smiled but caught myself when I realized she was serious. Without hesitation, she continued, "Koi fish cost $35 each!" Horrified at the cost, I momentarily pondered if CPR could be administered to fish. Thankfully, there was no need. We found the fish swimming between the crevices of the newly "placed" rocks. Apparently, none of the fish had suffered a heart attack.

Our forgiving neighbor accepted my profound apologies. My husband and I paid for the damages, and he helped restore the pond to its original state. In the process, however, I learned something noteworthy about koi fish. I learned that a small koi-fish placed in a small pond will always remain a small fish. But if that same small fish is placed in a large pond, it can grow up to two feet in length. A koi fish grows in proportion to the size of its pond.

So does our faith.

If God allows us to remain in the small, comfortable ponds of life, our faith will remain small. But in His wisdom and love, He often places us in the large overwhelming ponds of life where we experience unexpected trials and difficulties. While it seems contradictory to His goodness, it's in the large ponds that our faith is tested, and endurance is produced. It's here that others see the good work God is doing in us. It's in the large ponds that our faith grows.

Jairus knew Jesus could heal his dying daughter. Mary and Martha were confident of the Lord's healing abilities. But neither Jairus nor the sisters had any idea Jesus could raise the dead. While the pause for Jairus and the delay for Mary and Martha seem painfully unmerited, it is precisely in those places that their faith is being stretched. Certainly, they did not ask for a more mature faith. And certainly, when they took their request to Jesus, they could not have anticipated His ways.

Without considering the end of the story, imagine the mindset of Jairus when the unthinkable happens.

While He was still speaking, someone came from the house of the synagogue official, saying, "Your daughter has died; do not trouble the Teacher anymore." (Luke 8:49)

Can you feel the heartbreak of this once hopeful father? Can you hear his bewildered gasp when he receives the news his daughter has died? Can you see the tears of confusion streaming down his face? For Jairus, there seems to be an unwritten, painful suspension between the sorrow of verse 49 and the hope yet to come.

Verse 49 reminds me of my own heartbreak and confusion. When the doctor came to me in the hospital waiting room and said, "Your husband is nigh unto death," I replied through confident tears, "But we are praying." How could God do anything other than heal? How could the expectant prayers of hundreds of people gathered in the hospital waiting room go unheeded? Yet, just an hour later, I made the gut-wrenching decision to release my husband into God's care—the final click of the ventilator forever embedded in my mind.

Many of us have wrestled with disappointment. We have asked God, "Why?"—never receiving tidy answers that satisfy our broken hearts. Certainly, the Lord is compassionate toward the crushed in spirit (Psalm 34:18). He is patient with us when we question and wrestle, but ultimately, He desires for us to trust Him completely.

It seems that faith is often confused with theatrics— measured by bold claims, loud proclamations, or intense emotions. A mature Biblical faith, however, is simply trusting God enough to obey Him. If our faith lies in the healing we desire, the answers we claim, the miracles we expect, or the timing we anticipate; our faith will be shipwrecked when God chooses another way. Instead, He wants to develop our faith so that our focus is God Himself. A deep faith requires abandonment to Christ, not loud proclamations. It requires open hands, not fists that tightly grasp our own solutions.

Personally, I can attest to the fact that there are many things about God we cannot fully comprehend until we have lived, at least momentarily, on the edge of desperate. Left to our own devices, we would never venture into the large ponds where faith grows. We would never allow God to be glorified through our heartache. Like Jairus, we would be content with a healing while Jesus wants a resurrection.

Desperate Demonstrates God's Glory (Luke 8:50-56 and John 11:34-44)

After Jairus receives the devastating news that his daughter has died, Jesus speaks comfort, urging the grieving father to have faith. Indeed, Jairus has a measure of faith, which he had exercised in coming to Jesus with his request for healing. So, we must be careful as we read verse 50, *But when Jesus heard this, he answered him, "Do not be afraid any longer, only believe, and she shall be made well."* Jesus is not asking Jairus to muster up more faith. Jesus is asking Jairus to continue trusting Him. It is not the depth or size of Jairus' faith that will raise his daughter, rather it is the power of Almighty God demonstrated in Jesus Christ. The focus of Jairus' faith, not the depth of it, is where hope lies.

Jesus is moving Jairus from fear to faith, from anxious to amazed, from a finite view of God to an infinite one. He will move Mary and Martha in the same direction. While undoubtedly God is increasing their faith, He is also demonstrating His glory. He is using sorrow, pain, and discomfort to reveal His indisputable power over death. Jesus is not simply a healer; He is Lord over life and death. He is God in the flesh, far above anything Jairus, or the sisters, ever imagined.

The outcome for both Jairus' family and Lazarus' family are similar. Both families experience a resurrection that overwhelmingly glorifies God. Both families are changed forever. While the outcomes are similar, the approach that Jesus takes is unique for each situation.

Lazarus' resurrection is very public. There is a crowd of mourners, Jewish friends, family, disciples, and other followers of Jesus—all present at the tomb of Lazarus. Everything about the scene is bold and demonstrative. The removal of the stone from the opening of the tomb, the realization that Lazarus has been dead for four days, the size of the crowd, and the intense emotion of Jesus… all add to the anticipation of what is forthcoming. Jesus speaks with a loud voice, calling Lazarus from the grave. Shockingly, Lazarus emerges, wrapped in grave clothes. Everyone sees the miracle, and everyone is amazed. In fact, many believe in Jesus as the Messiah. Furthermore, Jesus gives no instruction to stay quiet about Lazarus' resurrection.

The resurrection of Jairus' daughter is different. There is no crowd inside the room where her body lies. The professional mourners have been dismissed. Only the girl's parents and three disciples accompany Jesus into the secluded room. The scene bares more tenderness than boldness. While Jesus speaks with authority, His tone and His actions reflect His ever-present compassion for children. He takes her small hand in His and calls to her, *"Child arise"* (Luke 8:54). Death releases her and life floods her young soul and body. Jesus tells the amazed parents to feed her and then firmly instructs them to tell no one of the event.

Two stories about resurrection. One bold, demonstrative, and public. One quiet, tender, and private. Both accounts result in life, but frankly most of us prefer the Lazarus approach when we are seeking God's intervention in our distress. We want God to come through with dramatic boldness. We want to

testify of the miraculous which changes everything suddenly...
at least that's what I wanted.

After my husband's car accident, he was transported to the
University of Tennessee Medical Center in Knoxville. While he
was in surgery, dozens of friends and family began to arrive at
the hospital. The numbers grew as the night stretched on. They
were there to encourage me, pray with me, and offer support,
but I just wanted to be alone. I wanted to find a quiet corner to
pray and read my Bible, hoping the Lord would speak to me,
giving me some clue about the outcome of this alarming night.
My desire for solitude wasn't going to happen, and it seemed in
the moment that God was dreadfully silent.

Of course, I didn't have my Bible with me. This was long
before iPhones and downloads of Scripture, but I was a Bible
teacher. I had memorized dozens of verses and passages of
Scripture. So while crowds of people circulated around me, I
began to scroll through my mind, trying to review Scripture.
Surely, the Holy Spirit would stop me at just the right verse
to bring hope and comfort into my distress and rising panic.
But not one verse came to my traumatized mind. Not a single
verse...until I heard a whisper...

"I am the resurrection and the life..."

I was familiar with this verse but never intentionally
memorized it. I didn't know the context, nor did I remember
why or to whom Jesus said it. I knew it was only a portion of a
passage, but which one? While there were unknowns about the
context of the phrase, I knew the voice who whispered it to me.
I knew this was my promise from God...and I grasped it. Yes, I
claimed it with all my heart. I fully believed my husband would
experience a healing that night. Life would be the winner.

Throughout the night, the Holy Spirit whispered again and again His promise to me, *"I am the resurrection and the life...."* While nurses scurried around my husband's bed, while doctors spoke to me with caution, while the ventilator clicked, while friends prayed, while some sang, while people around the globe joined the vigil...the very core of me continued to hear, *"I am the resurrection and the life."* Surely, at the end of this ordeal, we would glorify God. We would praise Him. We would testify. It would be our Lazarus moment! I believed it with all my heart.

Sadly, at one o'clock a.m. on September 27, 2005, my precious Dana left this earth and met Jesus face to face. The healing I anticipated didn't come.

In the hours between death and dawn, I was able to have those moments of solitude...just me and the Lord. I found the verse He had whispered to me throughout the night. It was John 11:25. Jesus is speaking to Martha after Lazarus has died. Martha is questioning Jesus' care and concern for her family. Jesus, however, redirects her disappointment to the truth of who He is. He redirected my disappointment as well. The entire verse reads:

Jesus said to her, "I am the resurrection and the life; he who believes in Me shall live even if he dies."

Do you see it? All night at the hospital, the Holy Spirit gave me only the first phrase of Jesus' words. With compassion, God's Spirit had been pointing me toward the person of Christ, not the outcome of events. My focus would always need to be Christ alone. He would be my hope, not my circumstances or my desired outcome or my anticipated timing.

The second phrase, *he who believes in me shall live even if he dies,* was gently given to me after Dana's death, in a moment of solitude at home. There was no crowd, no prayers, no singing. There was only Jesus, holding my trembling soul, assuring me that my husband was more alive than he had ever been. Dana received more than a healing. He received a great resurrection. He had a Lazarus moment, raised from death to be in the very presence of Christ forever. What a glorious day for Dana. What a powerful resurrection he experienced! Because Jesus is indeed the resurrection and the life, God was glorified that night…even as we grieved.

Looking back over the last eighteen years, I have experienced resurrection too. Like Jairus, mine has not been as bold and demonstrative as the resurrection of Lazarus. Mine has been quiet and private, no less miraculous, but perhaps less dramatic.

Every day since my husband's death, Jesus has quietly said to me, *"Child arise. Child arise… I see you. Child arise… I am providing for you. Child arise… I am fighting for you. Child arise… I am interceding for you. Child arise… I am working in the lives of your children. Child arise…I have a future for you."*

There have been many days I wanted a healing for myself and my children, for the pain of grief to go away, for the stress of life to subside—for God to fix it all. But I can say confidently the Lord has done a different kind of work in my life. While I have never received a dramatic resurrection, I have experienced a daily resurrection in Christ, a daily demonstration of His glory. Certainly, my life is different from what I had anticipated, but it is a very full life—filled with grace and hope, a life that has taken me deeper into the love of God than I ever asked to go.

Precious reader, what is your great need today? Are you taking your great need to the Lord? Are you taking your game plan as well? Will you trust Him to work in His way and in His time? Will you choose to remember God is always working, always sovereign, always leading us into truth? He is developing your faith, dear one, completing and maturing you in ways for which you never asked or imagined. He is revealing Himself to you in fresh ways, always in agreement with His Word. He will demonstrate His glory in you and through you...as you trust Him.

The edge of desperate is a daunting place we would never choose to visit, much less live. Yet it is here God Himself waits for us. While He is interested in our every need, He does more than repair our lives. He changes everything for our good and His glory. He redeems and matures, doing far more than we expected. He offers more than healing. He offers resurrection—abundant life in Christ—even while we live on the edge of desperate.

Discussion Questions
Desperate for Life

1. How has God used a desperate situation in your life for good? (Rom: 8:28) In what ways do you see God shaping your faith through this hardship?

2. When God's plans are different than your plans, what can you trust about the character of God? Read and discuss Isaiah 55:8-9. Are these difficult verses to embrace?

3. Our study emphasizes God's timing and our waiting. Give an example of a time that God used a season of waiting to accomplish spiritual growth in your life.

4. Have your emotions ever conflicted with the truth of God's goodness and love for you? Have your own expectations and your own definition of love ever been a hinderance to experiencing His care? Read Proverbs 3:5-6

5. Reread Psalm 77:7-13. Describe the writer's change in focus. Have God's promises ever changed your focus during a desperate time?

6. James 1:2-4 clearly reveals God's purpose in allowing trials in our lives. In your own words, what is His purpose for us in the trials of life? Have you experienced this in your life?

2

DESPERATE
For Purpose

Teaching college students in a weekly Bible study for twelve years presented joys and challenges to me. My late husband was pastoring a church in the same city as the University of Tennessee, and we were blessed to have a wonderful group of students join our congregation. Each week, those students kept me on my toes as I dug deep into God's Word, trying to apply truth to their needs and questions. Their sharp minds were always filled with eager ideas and sincere inquiries, especially when it came to understanding the will of God. During those twelve years, the most often asked question among our group of students was *"How can I know God's will for my life?"*

Perhaps every Christian has asked the same question and wrestled with a degree of uncertainty in the answer. Often, however, when we sincerely ask the Lord, *"What is Your will for my life?"* we want specific answers to specific questions. We want to know who to marry or date, where to live, what job to seek, or what to study. While all these questions are important, they are not the starting point. In fact, *"What is God's will for my life?"* is initially the wrong question.

Hang with me through this chapter. I am not interested in confusing you or discrediting honest questions. I do, however, want us to come to a clear understanding of God's will and how it applies to our lives.

Turning to Scripture for answers, Moses is a man who wrestled with the question of God's will for his life. In fact, he wrestled for the better part of his first eighty years. He would eventually learn that purpose must be God-centered, not self-centered. He also came to understand that his assignment could only be lived out through a deep and meaningful relationship with God.

The second chapter of Exodus is a synopsis of the first eighty years of Moses' life. God is at work from the very beginning. Certainly, his mother's bold actions to save baby Moses from Pharaoh's cruel edict and the events that unfold thereafter are evidence of God's sovereignty (Exodus 2:1-10). From infancy to adulthood, Moses grows up in Pharaoh's palace. He is highly educated, rigorously trained in military prowess, and well acquainted with both the religious and political mindset of Egypt. But Exodus 2:11 reveals a shift in Moses.

Moses is an adult. We don't know how much he knows about his Hebrew heritage. Neither do we know the depth of his knowledge of God or his full understanding of God's assignment for him. In Stephen's great sermon to the Jews (Acts 7:18-44), we are told that as an Egyptian prince, Moses is a man of great power and authority. *"But when he was approaching the age of forty, it entered his mind to visit his brethren, the sons of Israel"* (Acts 7:23). He is moved to anger when he sees a Hebrew being abused by an Egyptian. Acting on his own authority and in his own power, Moses kills the abusive Egyptian. Perhaps Moses has some inkling that he will deliver the Hebrews from bondage, but using his own authority to do it backfires. Moses flees the rage of Pharaoh and ends up on the backside of the desert—in the shadow of God's holy mountain. Far from both his Egyptian and Hebrew roots, he lives for forty years as a shepherd and family man... all the while, God is at work.

Like many of us, Moses is searching for meaning to life. While he has all the tools for success, somehow life has not come together as he expected. Exodus 3, however, highlights a dramatic turning point for Moses. Before the burning bush experience, Moses may have known *about* the Hebrew God, but in the desert of both Midian and life, Moses meets Yahweh—the God of his Hebrew father and the God of his Hebrew ancestors. Moses has a personal encounter with God Almighty and nothing will ever be the same.

Precious reader, you may have everything you need for success in this life and still fall short of contentment and purpose. The starting point is a personal encounter with God through His son Jesus Christ. Jesus is clear when He speaks to His disciples, *"I am the way, and the truth and the life; no one comes to the Father, but through Me"* (John 14:6). While our encounter with God may not be as dramatic as it was for Moses, it is no less miraculous.

Jesus is God in the flesh. He has come to show us the heart of God and to draw us to God the Father. God wants to have a personal relationship with you. He wants you to have more than an intellectual knowledge of Him. He desires far more than religion. Scripture tells us that sin separates us from God and the price of our sin is death. But God is so rich in mercy, and He loves us so much that He allowed His perfect son Jesus to die in our place, receiving the punishment for our sin. Like Moses, our relationship with God is initiated by God Himself. Our response is to humbly repent of sin and receive His free gift of new life through Jesus Christ. Also like Moses, when we encounter God through Christ, nothing will ever be the same.

God's Purpose

Scripture is God's story. It is easy to focus on the human characters that fill the pages of the Bible, but make no mistake, God is the focus. He is the overarching, indisputable center of everything. Therefore, His will—His purpose, His desire—is the center of everything as well. God's purpose is always God-centered. Isaiah 46:10 records God's own words about His will: *"... My purpose will be established, and I will accomplish all my good pleasure."* My friend Pastor Tony Plumber puts it this way. "The will of God is whatever God wants done, whatever He wants to accomplish, whatever brings Him joy, and whatever glorifies Him." This is a great working definition for us as we seek God's will. In this chapter you will notice that the phrases *will of God, purpose of God, desire of God, and heart of God* are used interchangeable.

Moses has an encounter with God at the foot of Mount Horeb. A burning bush in the arid wilderness of Midian grabs

Moses' attention. When Moses is drawn toward the bush, God immediately speaks, introducing Himself and establishing His holiness (Exodus 3:4-6). Moses responds in obedience and humility. While this is the beginning of Moses' relationship with God, God has known Moses before time began. God's holy plan, perfectly etched in history, will include Moses' participation. However, regardless of Moses' participation, God's purpose (His will) will be established, and God's purpose will remain God-centered.

In the context of relationship, God reveals His purpose to Moses. Notice as you read Exodus 3:7-8 the number of times God refers to Himself. Underline or circle the personal pronouns (me, my, and I) that refer to God as He reveals His plans to Moses.

And the Lord said, "I have surely seen the affliction of My people who are in Egypt and have given heed to their cry because of their taskmasters, for I am aware of their suffering. So, I have come down to deliver them from the power of the Egyptians, and to bring them up from that land to a good and spacious land, to a land flowing with milk and honey...." (Exodus 3:7-8a)

Everything in the Old Testament points us to the New Testament. God's gracious purpose revealed in verse eight *("**I have come down to deliver them** from the power of the Egyptians, and **to bring them up** from that land to a good and spacious land...")* is a foreshadowing of our salvation through Christ. The Apostle Paul writes a New Testament correlation to God's words in Exodus 3, *"For He delivered us from the domain of darkness and transferred us to the kingdom of His* *beloved Son, in whom we have redemption, and the forgiveness of sin"* (Colossians 1:13-14).

God is, and always has been, the Redeemer. He came down in power to redeem, to buy back, to set free, to deliver His people. The Hebrew people were delivered from the power of the Egyptians. You and I, along with every other New Testament believer, are delivered from the power (the domain) of sin. The outworking of His deliverance is a new life. For the Hebrews, their new life is in a good and plentiful land. For the Christian, it is an abundant life in Christ (John 10:10).

To the human mind the will of God is eternally complex, but at the heart of His will lies redemption. He has come down to bring us up—ultimately redeeming sinful people to live in communion with Him. Our response to the will of God is found in The Lord's Prayer: *"Your Kingdom come. Your will be done on earth as it is in heaven"* (Matthew 6:10). Even Jesus reminds His disciples that He has come down, not to do His own will, but to do the will of His Father (John 6:38). Again, God's purpose is God-centered, not man-centered. Initially, Moses gets that dynamic wrong, and, unfortunately, many times so do we.

After God clearly states His purpose to Moses, God invites Moses to join Him in the implementation of His purpose. *"Therefore, come now, and I will send you..."* (Exodus 3:10). Anytime God invites human beings to join His purpose, it is on the basis of grace. Indeed, our salvation is by grace (Ephesians 2:8-9), but also any good work or assignment God offers us is also based on His grace. Certainly, Moses has just met God. His relationship with God is new, and at best Moses' response to God's invitation is lacking in maturity. Moses misunderstands. He tries to make God's purpose of redeeming Israel all about himself, all about his own abilities.

The conversation that ensues between God and Moses is punctuated with self-centered questions and statements from Moses. Paraphrased... *Who am I?* (Exodus 3:11) *What will I say about You?* (Exodus 3:13) *What happens if they don't believe me?* (Exodus 4:1) *I'm not qualified* (Exodus 4:10). *Get someone else* (Exodus 4:13). Moses is asking the wrong questions and coming up with false assumptions. Consequently, God must redirect Moses' thinking from being self-centered to being God-centered. God's purpose is not dependent on Moses. God is simply inviting Moses to participate. It's not about Moses. It's all about God.

I have to admit I have struggled often with the question of God's will. However, most of my struggles have come when I add the phrase *for my life* to questions about God's will. Like Moses, for much of my life, I have viewed my relationship with God through a lens that focuses more on me than on God. I have read passages like Romans 12:2 and Colossians 1:9 and mistakenly believed that God's will is something that primarily speaks to *my job, my ministry, my activity, or my decisions.* Sadly, many other believers have fallen into the same trap— viewing God's purpose from a self-centered perspective.

God's will—His purpose—never requires our abilities. It requires our surrender. Therefore, our questions about God's will can no longer be *"What is God's will for my life?"* Instead, our first and foremost question must be *"What is God's will?"* This is not superficial semantics. This is not clever wording intended to confuse or condemn. To remove the phrase *for my life* from our questions about God's will and His purpose is a shift in our thinking—moving us away from our selfish inclination to see things only as they pertain to us while moving us toward seeing all of life from God's perspective.

Certainly, God cares about everything in our lives. He wants to be involved in the huge life-changing decisions we must make, as well as the choices that intersect each moment of the day. He wants us to pray, to inquire, to seek answers to our questions, but if we are self-focused in our seeking, we will miss the heart of God.

As He did with Moses, God is inviting us to know Him. Every question we may have about our own lives is secondary to knowing the heart of God. As we become intimately acquainted with God, our questions begin to change. Our desires change as well. We begin to see all of life, not just our individual lives, from His perspective. His heartbeat becomes our heartbeat, and His purpose becomes our purpose as well.

Joining God's Purpose

As a believer in Christ, our primary purpose is to know God. Any assignment, job, ministry, or task which God may provide is a subpoint to our primary purpose of knowing Him. God created us for relationship with Him, and that relationship is always on the basis of grace. As New Testament believers, certainly we can attest to salvation by grace through Christ. Grace, however, is also the only means of relationship with God in the Old Testament.

God did not meet Moses at the foot of Mount Horeb because Moses was the best and brightest or the most deserving guy around. God initiated a relationship with imperfect, possibly hot-headed, insecure Moses based on God's grace—undeserved, unlimited grace. As we read beyond that first awkward, rather self-focused conversation Moses has with God, the rest of Exodus (also Leviticus, Numbers, and

Deuteronomy) is filled with two notable phrases: *The Lord said to Moses* and *Moses said to the Lord.* These phrases speak of a deep and ongoing relationship between Moses and God. Notice, God never sacrifices His holiness. He remains the Almighty, Yahweh, and The Great I AM even while pursuing a relationship with Moses. God chooses, by grace, *to speak to Moses face to face as a man speaks to a friend* (Exodus 33:11).

Any assignment God gives to Moses flows out of relationship. Relationship comes first. Moses will never successfully do anything for God until he first knows God intimately.

You and I will never have clarity or direction in our lives until we make relationship with God a priority. Our purpose must align with His purpose. In fact, we have no meaningful purpose apart from God's purpose. Without an intimate knowledge of God through Jesus Christ, our well-meaning plans will be short-sighted and empty of eternal fruit. We cannot bypass intimacy with the Lord in favor of activity for the Lord.

Certainly, God is interested in what we do with our time here on earth. He cares about every desire of our heart, but He is more concerned that our desires reflect His heart. Psalm 37:4 says, *"Delight yourself in the Lord and He will give you the desires of your heart."* We tend to read that verse with our own happiness in mind and the false assumption that God will do whatever we want Him to do.

The first phrase of Psalm 37:4 sheds light on the second phrase. *Delight yourself in the Lord* has nothing to do with happiness. In this verse the word *delight* means to be *conformed.* As we intentionally draw near to God, always responding to His invitation for relationship, His Holy Spirit conforms us to Christ. He changes our desires to reflect His desires. When our desires look like His desires, THEN He gives us the desires of our hearts.

So how do we intentionally draw near to Him? How can we have more than a religious or intellectual knowledge of our Redeemer? How can we know His purpose and then align our lives with it? Certainly, we have been invited into this relationship with Christ, but do we understand that it is an ongoing, ever- deepening intimacy with Him?

The Apostle Paul wanted Christians to know God intimately and to experience the abundant life in Christ. Within his letters to the church, Paul fervently prays for the Holy Spirit to open their spiritual eyes so that they understand the value of their relationship with Christ. Colossians 1:9-12 is one of Paul's prayers for the church. As you read the following verses, notice what Paul does not pray. He does not pray for larger churches, better financial opportunities, or rigorous health. He says nothing of personal power, position, prestige, or material possessions. Everything in Paul's prayer hinges on the phrase *...that you may be filled with the knowledge of His will.*

*For this reason also, since the day we heard of it, we have not ceased to pray for you and to ask **that you may be filled with the knowledge of His will** in all spiritual wisdom and understanding, so that you may walk in a manner worthy of the Lord, to please Him in all respects, bearing fruit in every good work and increasing in the knowledge of God, strengthened with all power according to His glorious might, for the attaining of all steadfastness and patience, joyously giving thanks to the Father who has qualified us to share in the inheritance of the saints in light.* (Colossians 1:9-12)

56

In the original language, these four verses are all one sentence, each phrase building upon the preceding phrase. For the next few pages let's dig into each phrase and follow Paul's train of thought.

...we have not ceased to pray for you and to ask that you be filled with the knowledge of His will...

To be *filled* means to be *controlled by.* In this context, knowledge means far more than intellectual information or common sense. Biblical knowledge is truth that we intentionally embrace and participate in. We are to know His will, completely yield ourselves to His will, and fully participate in His will. Knowing His will includes knowing God's ways, His heart, and His character. Be careful with this verse. I misunderstood it for many years. It is not saying "be filled with a knowledge of His will *for my life.*"

...in all spiritual wisdom and understanding...

Wisdom is the application of truth. *Understanding* is the ability to appraise or determine the value of something. The knowledge of God's will must be spiritually applied to our circumstances. Human reasoning cannot adequately apply Biblical truth to our circumstances—only the Holy Spirit can do that.

In the simplest of terms, we must know the heart of God and allow His desires to guide and direct everything about our lives. However, we will never know His heart, we will never live out His purpose, we will never have wisdom or understanding about these deep and intimate spiritual matters apart from God's Word.

The Bible is God's greatest tool for revealing to us His purpose. We know God's will, and we are able to apply it to our circumstances to the degree we yield to His Word. God's wisdom and God's will are inseparable from God's Word. Moses prayed, *"Teach me Your ways that I might know You"* (Exodus 33:13). We are free to pray the same thing with our Bibles open and our minds tuned to hear Him speak.

...so that you may...

Being filled with the knowledge of His will has a practical outcome. It changes the way we live. Colossians 1:9 flows right into Colossians 1:10. The words *so that* in verse 10 are connecting words, like a needle and thread stringing phrases together. The knowledge of His will is tied to the way we live our lives.

...walk in a manner worthy of the Lord...

Paul often uses the word *walk* to refer to daily living. It makes sense. Most of life is not a sprint; it is a one-step-at-a-time walk. If our walk is spiritually consistent and in balance with God's will, there will be good results. *To walk in a manner worthy of the Lord* (verse 10) simply means to live in perfect balance with His desires, always mindful to please Him in everything we do and say...and yes, even in everything we think. Rest assured; our actions are not earning us extra favor from God. We have His favor in full simply because we are His children. However, when our actions are aligned with His heart, our lives bear good fruit.

...bearing fruit in every good work...

Paul is using the word fruit metaphorically, just as Jesus does in John 15. *"I am the vine, you are the branches; he who abides in Me and I in him, he bears much fruit; for apart from*

Me you can do nothing" (John 15:5). Fruit is any beneficial work that glorifies God. A beneficial work can be our words, our worship, our occupation, our relationships, our ministry, our daily interaction with people, our prayers....do you get the idea? God can bring good fruit out of everything in our lives when we are living to please Him.

...increasing in the knowledge of God...

Interestingly, as we live to please Christ and bear good fruit, we also increase in our *knowledge of God*. Paul has come back around to knowledge of God. Again, Paul is not referring to book knowledge. Knowing God is a relationship that spans our entire life. Our relationship will deepen and mature the more we understand the loving heart of our Savior, the more we yield to Him, the more we live to please Him. We do not live this way to gain a relationship with God. We live this way because we already have a relationship with Him through Jesus.

...strengthened with all power...

Encouraging words continue to flow from Paul's prayer. Colossians 1:11 assures us that the power source for godly living is God Himself. We have His Holy Spirit dwelling within us, empowering us to live as God has commanded us to live. All of our walking worthy, bearing fruit in every good work, and increasing in the knowledge of God is fueled by the Holy Spirit. Our job is to yield and participate—to trust and obey.

...for the attaining of all steadfastness and patience...

Steadfastness is defined as patient enduring. It is a quality that does not surrender to circumstances. Steadfastness and patience are characteristics of a mature believer: one who knows God intimately, trusts Him completely, and lives for Him wholeheartedly. Jeremiah 17:7-8 beautifully describes the mature, steadfast believer.

They are like trees planted along a riverbank, with roots that reach deep into the water. Such trees are not bothered by the heat or worried by long months of drought. Their leaves stay green and they never stop producing fruit. (Jeremiah 17:7-8 NLT)

...joyously giving thanks to the Father...

Even as I type, I am reminded again of all that God has done for us in Christ. I find myself joyfully—even tearfully—giving thanks. As we read Paul's prayer, line by line, somewhere along the way we begin to sense overwhelming joy and gratitude that leads to humble worship.

...who has qualified us...

Our thankfulness stems from the liberating truth that relationship with God does not rest in our own good works. No great ministry, no moral lifestyle, no honorable service, no valiant work, nor big ideas for God can qualify us to be His children. We are qualified on the basis of His grace. Scripture assures us that salvation is by grace through faith in Jesus Christ. *For by grace you have been saved through faith; and that not of yourselves, it is a gift of God; not as a result of works, that no one should boast* (Ephesians 2:8-9). When we know Christ, we become part of the family of God, sharing in the wealth of God's goodness.

As we have examined Paul's prayer for the church, would you read it again? Would you personalize it by inserting your name or the names of your loved ones? In my Bible, I have written the names of my children and grandchildren in the margin beside these powerful verses in Colossians. Certainly, I have prayed for God's blessings for my loved ones—for His peace, for wisdom, for healing, for daily needs to be met. Certainly, I have cried out at times for God's intervention in crisis and tragedy and sickness. Most assuredly, I have laid our brokenness before the throne of grace. But through the years, God has continued pressing me to pray with urgency that they would know and love God and that they would live to please Him in every way.

Dear reader, pray about everything on your heart, but first pray for a knowledge of His will applied to your life in wisdom and understanding so that your daily walk reflects Christ. Joining our lives to His purpose is life-changing and liberating. It also prepares us to receive any assignment God offers.

Receiving God's Assignments

At the burning bush, God firmly establishes a relationship with Moses and subsequently tells Moses His plans for redeeming Israel. After establishing a relationship and after conveying His will for Israel, God invites Moses to participate in the plans of God. God gives Moses an assignment—a unique opportunity that will further God's eternal purpose. God sends Moses back to Egypt to be a spokesperson for God and a catalyst for Israel's release from slavery. The assignment continues for Moses' entire life as he leads Israel to their new home in the promised land. Moses' assignment, however, is always anchored in relationship with God and in an ever-deepening knowledge of God's ways (Exodus 33:13).

I want you to understand the sequence of events: relationship with God, an ever-deepening knowledge of God's purpose, and, finally, assignment from God. In our own lives, we must not get this sequence out of order. We cannot ask the Lord for an assignment, a ministry, or a personal purpose until we know God through Jesus Christ and we are willing to link our lives with His purpose.

Certainly, the Lord has a plan for your life—an assignment that is meaningful and fulfilling. But, dear one, He wants us to love Him deeply and surrender to Him completely. He doesn't need our big ideas or our well-laid plans. He wants us to trust Him enough to say yes to anything He might ask of us. Our "yes" to the Lord begins with our daily obedience to Him. I have found that obedience comes easier when I know and trust His heart—when I set aside my own desires and daily embrace whatever pleases Him. Pastor Tony Evans poignantly addresses the issue of trust. He is quoted in Henry Blackaby's book, *Experiencing God.*

Whenever I enter a contract with anyone, they usually ask me to sign on the bottom line. What that usually means is that I know the terms and conditions of the contract. Like this contractor, we too often give God a full page of activities we are going to do for Him and ask Him to sign off on it. Instead, God gives us a blank sheet of paper for us to sign on the bottom line, demonstrating our trust in Him and His will for our lives. The question is not, "Will God sign off on what we want to do?" but rather "Will we trust God to do what He wants done?" (296)

Knowing and trusting God prepares us for receiving any assignment God offers. We don't need to come up with grand ideas and present them to the Lord for His approval. Instead, every day is an opportunity to serve Christ, to walk closely with Him, and to live with an acute awareness that He is always at work. Keep in mind that our relationship with Christ is not a nebulous, esoteric experience. There are Biblical principles, perimeters, and practicalities to guide us as we seek to serve Christ. I have listed a few that are meaningful to me.

God initiates all assignments. I have written it twice already: God does not need or want our big ideas. He has not asked us to use our imaginations, and certainly not our selfish motives, to come up with something that will make a big impact in the world. Remember, Moses had a big idea for God. He ended up killing an Egyptian and then running for his life. Moses' plan for taking care of God's people was not God's plan. It is important for us to remember: *God's assignments are received, not achieved.*

Hebrews 11 is often nicknamed *The Hall of Faith*. Every person listed in Hebrews 11 had a profound impact on people and events. Each person listed is an example of living by faith. But not one person presented in Hebrews 11 came up with their own idea for serving God. Instead, God gave each person instructions in the form of a call or an assignment. In response, each person trusted God and obeyed. Each person responded in faith. Faith is not a leap into the dark, neither is it bold and dramatic claims. Faith is trusting God enough to obey Him.

As we know the Lord more intimately, our faith matures. He will lead us into the good and beneficial work prepared for us (Ephesians 2:10, Colossians 1:10). This life on earth is not simply Heaven's waiting room; rather, each day is an opportunity to listen to the Holy Spirit and obey Him.

Assignments may or may not be a vocational call to ministry. Usually, God's assignments are given in the context of everyday living as we are following Christ daily. The work He has for us is often an outgrowth of what we are already doing or relationships we already have. Certainly, for some, God may have an assignment that requires a vocational change, a need for specialized training, or a move to another city or even another country. He may require some to leave everything and follow Him into a vocational ministry—but for most of us, the Lord uses us right where we are.

Recently, my husband Allen was asked to be a volunteer coach for our local high school varsity baseball team. Allen loves sports of any kind and was excited about the opportunity to work with young athletes. He was also thrilled to work alongside his friend Craig, who is the head baseball coach.

Craig has been a teacher and head baseball coach in our city for over twenty-five years. He has a reputation as a no-nonsense coach who turns out winning teams year after year. He was recently honored for 500 career wins ,and he has been inducted into the Florida High School Coach's Hall of Fame. Beyond any accolades, Craig is a Christian who believes that investing in the lives of young men is a high honor. Through the years, dozens of young athletes and many of their family members have come to know Jesus Christ through the influence of Craig. God has given Craig an assignment, right here where he lives and works. The assignment is to be a light for Christ on the baseball field and in the community. The assignment is a natural overflow of Craig's love for the Lord and his love of coaching.

The Gospel of Luke tells the story of a man possessed with many demons. He lives an isolated and tormented life…

until he meets Jesus. By the end of the story, the man is healed and sitting at the feet of Jesus, clothed and in his right mind. Thankful for his healing, the man begs to join Jesus' entourage of disciples (Luke 9:26-39). Keep in mind, Jesus' twelve disciples were men whom Jesus called to leave everything and follow Him. The once demon-possessed man wanted to live daily in the company of Jesus and His band of disciples. In today's lingo we might say this thankful, redeemed man wanted to go into full-time Christian ministry. But Jesus said *no*.

Instead of leaving everything behind to follow Jesus, the man was told to go home and tell the great things done for him. *Go home and tell?* To our modern ears that sounds so anticlimactic after such an extraordinary redemption. Wouldn't Jesus have been better served if the man went with Jesus, testifying daily of his healing, showing the scars of his former life, and demonstrating the joy of his new life?

Scripture never tells us the degree of impact the once-possessed man had on his family and community. Scripture simply tells us of his obedience to go home and tell (Luke 9:39). Likewise, God may ask us to stay where we are and serve Him faithfully. He could also invite us to serve Him in a unique capacity or through a vocational ministry. Rest assured when God asks us to participate in His purpose, our response to His words *go home and tell* will require just as much faith as our response to His call *leave everything and follow Me*.

There are no small assignments. We live in a world that celebrates success. Even the church has a tendency to tout successful programs, eloquent teachers, growing congregations, best-selling authors, and wide-spread ministries. Christians have been told to *change the world, claim great things for God,* *or make a big impact*. But it seems we have narrowed spiritual success to results that can be measured and displayed. Don't get me wrong! Success can indeed be God-focused and God-empowered. Spiritual success can also be very motivating to others. I fear many times our definition of success is shaped by the world's definition of success, and, sadly, it has left most of us feeling like we are a big disappointment to God.

God initiates every assignment. He ordains the good and beneficial work that we participate in *for His glory.* He alone determines the scope and eternal impact of every assignment. His standard of measure is not like ours; consequently, we may never fully comprehend the eternal impact of our assignment, let alone be able to measure and display the results.

Jesus told His followers to *make disciples as they go* (Matthew 28:19). Likewise, you and I must be *as we go* followers of Christ. We cannot sit on our hands waiting for the "big assignment." We are to yield to Him daily, aware that He is constantly at work around us, always listening and ready to respond to His invitation to join His purpose. He may ask us to love and serve our neighbors, or He may ask us to take the gospel to the ends of the earth. God is the one who gives the assignments; therefore, no assignment is small, and every assignment has eternal impact.

In my book *Women of Grace*, I wrote at length about my maternal grandparents, Bill and Opal Mattheiss. They were married for over fifty years, raising eight children and influencing dozens of grandchildren, great- grandchildren, friends, neighbors, and fellow church members. Bill and Opal's generational influence was rooted in their love for Christ and their willingness to serve Him faithfully. Remarkably, most of their service took place within a five-mile radius of their home—service to their family, in their community, and through their local church. My grandparents never considered themselves professional ministers, and they were never paid for their tireless service. They simply embraced God's assignment one day at a time. I'm sure they never envisioned the godly legacy they were establishing in their family which continues today. Neither did they envision the ripples of influence for the gospel that have literally circled the globe. I thought of my grandparents when I recently read a quote used by Susan Narjala. "Almost everything in life that truly matters will require you to do small things, mostly overlooked things, over a long period of time with Him."

God's assignments will require something of us. Moses wrestled with God's assignment. Remember? He asked all those self-focused questions and doubted his own ability to accomplish what God was asking of him (Exodus 3-4). Moses was indeed given an assignment much larger than his own abilities. Even though Moses was highly educated and significantly trained, he could never accomplish on his own what God was asking of him. He would have to trust God, leaning solely on the Almighty to empower and provide. Moses would also have to make major adjustments and changes to his life in order to carry out God's assignment. Our assignments will also require trust as well as adjustments.

God always gives an assignment that is beyond our own abilities or outside our comfort zone. Because of that, God's assignments will almost always create a wrestling within us. While most of us want to trust and obey the Lord, we also want to set the boundaries. We want to tell God how much we are willing to change or give up. We want to formulate the game plan. We want to determine the amount of time and resources the assignment will cost us. In other words, we want control.

Our wrestling, our plans, our boundaries, and our control must give way to surrender. The Apostle Paul gives us a clearer understanding of surrender when he describes himself as a *bondservant* (Philippians 1:1). A *bondservant* is one who is in a permanent relationship of servitude, his will lost in the will of the master.

Like Paul, we are servants of Jesus Christ. *Surrender* is an abandonment of our plans, our resources, and, most definitely, our will. Be assured, God is not the cosmic killjoy, stomping out our heart's desires or thwarting our well-laid plans. Rather, He is doing more than we ever asked or imagined. He has an eternal purpose we cannot fully grasp; therefore, we must trust His heart and yield to Him in obedience. We may not clearly see the path He will take or understand how He will accomplish the assignment through us. However, when we surrender to Him, there is a joy and contentment which supersedes the discomfort and questions we initially experience. We hand Him the blank piece of paper with our signature at the bottom—signing off on anything He asks of us.

God will equip you for any assignment He gives you. God equips Moses with everything he needs in order to accomplish anything God asks of him. Before Moses takes one step back to Egypt, God equips him. Be careful as you read Exodus 4. A cursory reading will lead us to believe there is power in Moses' staff or in the signs he is able to perform. The staff and the signs are tools. The power, however, is God Himself working through Moses. Without the power and presence of God, the staff is just a piece of wood and the signs are just a bag of tricks (Exodus 7:8-12).

God equips us to live as He commands us to live. He also equips us to serve. Our equipping comes through the Holy

Spirit of God living within us. At the moment of salvation, the Holy Spirit of Christ indwells the believer. He is our source of power for both life and service (John 14:16-17, Acts 1:8, Ephesians 3:16).

We are given spiritual gifts for the work of service and the building up of the church (Ephesians 4:12). Spiritual gifts are from the Holy Spirit. They are different from natural talents and abilities. Interestingly, God often fuses our natural abilities, training, personalities, and passions with our spiritual gifts. But make no mistake—it is the Holy Spirit within us who is the power source.

The Lord may give us opportunities for education and learning. He may provide friends and mentors to encourage and help us. He may enhance our lives with experiences and opportunities. However, no matter how many people or resources are at our disposal, they are, at best, limited without the presence of the Holy Spirit dwelling within us, equipping us for every good work.

God is always in charge of fruit. Years ago, when I organized my teaching and travels under the ministry title *Word of Joy, Inc.*, I was given a lot of advice about how to "increase" my ministry. I was told I needed a blog, a website, and a social media page. Some advised that I should get the word out about my ministry through marketing, mailouts, and self-promotion. Others suggested podcasts and livestreams. The advice continued to pour in when I wrote my first book. While there was nothing wrong with any of the advice given to me, I found myself spinning too many plates and coming up short on energy and peace.

I temporarily paused from all the activity of ministry to take stock of where God seemed to be working most. While trying to discern what aspects of ministry God was blessing without my frantic and exhausting efforts, I began to see the most beneficial and lasting results in two or three areas of my ministry. As I focused the majority of my time and energy on those areas, God began to increase the fruitful outcomes even more. I discovered that greater effort on my part could not produce lasting fruit. Only the Lord produces fruit, and according to John 15, my participation in bearing fruit starts and ends with *abiding in Christ and allowing His Word to abide in me.*

In the final hours before the crucifixion, Jesus stresses to His disciples the importance of abiding. He uses the metaphor of a vineyard to illustrate the connection between abiding in Him and bearing spiritual fruit. He uses the word abide ten times in the first eleven verses of John 15. Any time a word is repeated in a passage of Scripture, we would do well to take note of it.

To abide means *to settle down and live; to make a place your permanent home; to remain united in heart, mind and will; to persevere and remain steadfast.* Jesus says we are to abide in Him and allow His words to abide in us (John 15:7). Abiding in Christ is a relationship motivated by love and nourished by Scripture. Abiding in Christ cultivates within us a rich communion with Him far surpassing any emotional experience.

When I was a young pastor's wife, God gave me a beautiful picture of abiding through an older couple in our church. Their tender and loving relationship cultivated over sixty years of marriage still speaks volumes of what it means *to abide.*

Ray and Georgia Merritt were a humble senior adult couple who graced our East Tennessee congregation. When I met them, they were well into their seventies, maybe even their eighties. They were quiet and reserved with nothing flashy or superficial about either of them. Most notably, they were always together.

Ray was a retired carpenter. Since we had a bedroom closet door that needed some attention, my husband asked Ray if he would come by our house and look at it. Ray was happy to help. A few days later, his car pulled into our driveway. He gathered his tools, and then walked to the passenger side of the car to open the door for Georgia.

Truthfully, I wasn't expecting Georgia. Upon seeing her, I imagined she and I would sip iced tea in the kitchen while Ray worked. I watched them walk hand in hand up my driveway before opening the front door to greet them both. "Ray, I see you brought your assistant!" Georgia looked at me in bewilderment and gently replied, "Oh no, I'm not his assistant. I just love to be with Ray."

Ray worked on the closet door, but Georgia and I did not drink iced tea in the kitchen. She sat in the bedroom with Ray, just watching him work. I'm not sure they even had a conversation. Oh, she may have held the ladder or handed him a tool, but that wasn't why she was there. He was perfectly capable of doing the job by himself. Georgia simply wanted to be with Ray. And it seemed to me, Ray delighted in her company.

Abiding in Christ cannot be narrowed down to a block of time each day. It cannot be reduced to a formula. It is not a box to check off in our daily list of things to do. It is a relationship that permeates our being and saturates every thought, every word, and every action. As we abide in Christ, through His Word and through prayer, we become united with the heart, mind, and will of God. Out of this intimate relationship, God brings forth fruit in our daily lives. As I learned early in my ministry, we can muster up a few results in our own strength, but we cannot produce lasting fruit. Only God can do that, and He does it as we learn to abide.

Seeking God's Direction in Our Decisions

While Moses was given the assignment of leading God's people out of slavery and into the Promised Land, it stands to reason there were practical, daily decisions he had to make in the process. Likewise, as we walk daily with Christ, we will have to make decisions all along the way. How do we do that? How do we discern the heart of God in both small and large decisions—decisions we are faced with every single day? To me, this is where sincere questions like *who to marry, what to study, where to live, or which car to buy* come into play.

As believers in Christ, we are not free to wing it. We are not free to follow our hearts or our gut feelings when making decisions. We are, however, given Biblical principles to follow when making decisions. God is always at work, and He uses four things to guide us as we make decisions: ***His Word. His Spirit. His people. Our circumstances.***

His Word. The Bible is God's Word to us. I wrote earlier in this chapter: we cannot separate the will of God from the Word of God. We will never know the mind and heart of our Lord if we neglect His Word. That's why it is so important to not only just read Scripture, but also memorize it, meditate on it, sing it, write it down...any means that helps get it into our lives. As we plant God's Word into our minds, it creates a storehouse of truth. In times of decision-making, God will draw from that storehouse to remind us of specific truth that applies to our need. His Word is a lamp to our feet and a light to our path (Psalm 119:105). With His Word, He directs our steps. Listen carefully! If our heart tells us one thing and God's Word says something different, our heart is wrong! God will never, never lead us contrary to His Word.

His Spirit. We have already touched on the indwelling of the Holy Spirit. He is our source of strength to live the Christian life. He is also our Helper (John 14:16-17). As our Helper, He teaches us (John 14:26). His primary teaching tool is the Bible. The writer of Hebrews tells us the Word of God is active and alive, accomplishing its purpose in us. It is alive and active because the Holy Spirit infuses it with life. Using God's Word, the Spirit leads us into truth (John 16:13). God's Spirit may prompt us to move in a certain direction. He may prompt us to seek counsel. He may work in a hundred different ways, but rest assured—His leading will never contradict God's Word.

Additionally, as we seek the will of God in daily decisions, the Holy Spirit gives peace. Peace is the greatest indicator that we are moving in the right direction. The Apostle Paul refers to peace that surpasses understanding (Philippians 4:6-7). Even when life feels like an unsolvable puzzle, the Holy Spirit gives an unexplainable peace, which comforts and guards us as we seek God's direction for our lives.

Likewise, lack of peace is an indicator. Dozens of times in my own life I have been excited about a project, relationship, or opportunity only to find myself restless and uncertain as I moved forward—a sense of peace markedly absent. Lack of peace may simply be an indicator that the timing is not right. It can also be a red flag telling us to stop and wait until we have clear direction from the Lord.

Be careful here. Peace or lack of peace is not a feeling or emotion. Peace is from the Holy Spirit. You may still have unanswered questions and shaky knees as you move forward, but as you spend time abiding in Christ and allowing His Word to abide in you, you will learn to recognize God's peace.

His people. A dozen faces come to mind as I type these sentences. God's people have been a source of encouragement to me throughout my life. Through the years, I have been blessed with wise family members, friends, and teachers who have spoken truth into my life, helping me discern God's leading. For all of us, it matters which voices we allow to speak into our lives.

As we seek help from others, we must remember again the principles of abiding in Christ. When we abide, we learn what His wisdom sounds like. We know His heart. We become familiar with His nature and character. Therefore, when people speak into our lives, we recognize immediately if their words align with God. We cannot separate the Word of God from the wisdom of God, especially as we evaluate the counsel or advice that comes from other people.

People, even godly people, cannot have the final say in our decision-making process. Certainly, their words can have bearing on our decisions, helping us gain better understanding of ourselves or a situation. Scripture tells us, *"Get all the advice and instruction you can, so you will be wise the rest of your life"* (Proverbs 19:20 NLT). At the end of the day, however, you must be able to evaluate what is wise advice. You must also be able to prudently apply that counsel to your circumstances with a keen awareness of God's peace.

Our circumstances. God is always at work in the practical circumstances of our lives. He will use our circumstances to guide us into His plans. Our responsibility is to abide daily in Him and to build a rich storehouse of His Word in our minds.

We are also responsible to look around and see where God is already working in our relationships, our home, and our work.

God almost always begins working in our lives right where we are. He works incrementally and practically, laying solid foundations as we abide daily in Him. As we seek to obey Him and please Him each day, He opens doors of opportunity one at a time, in His time. While we are working and serving, we begin to sense what gives us the most joy and satisfaction. We start to recognize our talents, gifts, and abilities. We begin to naturally lean into the very thing He designed for us. If you want to know what to do next, do what is right in front of you now!

When my late husband died, I was uncertain about the next steps for my family. A dear friend called to check on me. In the conversation, I shared with her my confusion. She said something so simple, yet so profound. "Jennifer, do what you have always done." I knew exactly what she meant. While I could not change my circumstances, I could continue abiding in Christ. I could pray, seek counsel, and look to see what doors God was opening or closing. I could get up and take care of my boys, tending to the daily needs of my family. And I could wait for peace. This is how I had lived life before my husband's death, and this is how I could continue living even in the unexpected circumstances. Looking back, it astounds me how graciously the Lord has directed my steps.

As you review the four things God will use to guide you as you make decisions, I want to remind you of a few things— some I am still learning and some I am still wrestling with.

God is not micromanaging us. He is not looking over our shoulder, waiting to condemn us for making an imperfect decision. In fact, very few times in my life have I been completely certain I was making an absolutely perfect decision. I simply sensed a peace and had to trust God with the outcome.

We serve a loving, gracious God. He knows our limitations and our flaws. He understands that we cannot see around every corner; we do not know what the days ahead hold; we cannot foresee the effects or consequences of every decision we make. Rest, dear one, rest. There is grace in it all. Of course, His grace is not permission to live sloppy or rebellious lives, but it is a place to trust His heart as we move forward in our limited understanding of the future.

You might be thinking, "But what if I really mess up?" Precious reader, God is always at work, even in our shortsighted decisions, even in our uncertain steps, even in our failures. His love and His sovereignty always overshadow our limited humanity. Never forget, however, sinful choices have consequences. But God works even the consequences of sin for our good and His glory (Romans 8:28).

Additionally, as we seek to make decisions that please God, we must trust Him when He says, *"No."* Even if it doesn't make sense in the moment, even if it momentarily hurts, or even if it reshapes our plans, His *no* is for our good. He is protecting us from things we cannot see, and He is guiding us into something better suited for His purpose.

Allow me to finish this chapter about purpose just as I began it—with those beloved university students in Tennessee.

We moved to East Tennessee in 1992. My late husband, Dana, had been a student pastor for years, but this would be his first position as senior pastor. As the new pastor's wife, I assumed my role would primarily be teaching and serving women. I had been a women's Bible study leader in our previous church, and I was looking forward to building on that experience.

God had other plans.

Just a few months after arriving in Tennessee, a student from the University of Tennessee named Nathan attended our church on a Sunday evening. The church was not in close proximity to the University, neither did we have a thriving college ministry. Nathan had heard there was a new pastor in town, and on his own, decided to check things out. The next Sunday, Nathan returned to our church bringing with him a friend named Buffy. Nathan and Buffy would be the spark God used to start a fire.

In the weeks that followed, other students from the University of Tennessee began to attend our church—most of them were friends of Nathan and Buffy. My husband Dana was a natural magnet for students, but the only thing we had going for them at church was a Sunday morning Bible study. However, as the Sunday morning class grew, the husband and wife leading the class unexpectedly stepped down. No church member volunteered to take their place. In the absence of a teacher/leader for the growing number of university students, my husband began to pray.

On a Sunday evening, Dana called the entire church into a time of prayer. He asked all of us to come to the altar and pray for God to raise up a teacher for that growing class of university students. Wanting the best for our church and being a dutiful pastor's wife, I went to the front of the church with everyone else. I knelt at the steps leading up to the pulpit— but I wasn't praying. I was formulating in my mind a list of people who might be great leaders for the students. I planned to present my list to my husband, quite sure someone from my well-thought-out list would emerge as the teacher.

On that Sunday evening, while in the posture of prayer, formulating a list of potential teachers, the Holy Spirit interrupted my plans and clearly said to me, *"You teach that class."* It wasn't an audible voice. It wasn't a specific verse from the Bible that suddenly came to my mind. It was simply the urging and nudging of the Holy Spirit within me, telling me to teach a Sunday morning class already filled with university students. I flatly said, "No!"

Right there at the altar, I had a wrestling match with God. After all, I was a women's ministry leader. Teaching and working with women was my heart's desire. It was also my past experience. I wasn't equipped to teach university students. In fact, their intellect and curiosity frightened me. Certainly, I wasn't smart enough to tackle a room full of students. I finally sighed in agreement but foolishly stated to the Lord my boundaries and conditions for teaching.

Later that same night, I told my husband about my wrestling match with God. I also told my husband I would be happy to teach the Sunday morning Bible study class for college students… but only until God raised up another leader to take my place. Sometimes, it's humorous to look back and recall my conditions to God's instructions.

I taught college students for twelve years.

What a glorious twelve years God gave to our church and gave to me. He used those years to mature my teaching and deepen me in His Word. God instilled a discipline in me that had never existed: a discipline to study week in and week out, month after month, year after year. I learned more than I could ever convey in the classroom. Additionally, the Lord was strengthening my faith for difficult days ahead which I could not foresee.

God was working in students as well. Over the course of twelve years, hundreds of university students graced our church. Our church loved them well and the students provided a vibrancy that inspired and encouraged our congregation. Today, I am able to follow many of those students on social media. Some are pastors, student ministers, missionaries, and teachers. Some are testaments of faith in the business world. Many have married and raised families to honor and serve Christ. None of us will ever fully understand the eternal impact those students have had for God's Kingdom.

Listen carefully, dear reader. Dana and I were abiding in Christ long before we arrived in East Tennessee. Yes, we were young with much to learn, but our hearts were set on knowing and loving God—that was our purpose! Out of our ongoing relationship with Christ came a wonderful assignment to serve a church and, in particular for me, to serve college students. The assignment to teach students was not my big idea for God. God initiated it. The assignment was in the context of the church we were already serving. While it did not grow into a nationally recognized ministry or spawn a best-selling book about student ministry, it has had world-wide impact through the students who passed through our church. God has always been in charge of the spiritual fruit from those years, and He will continue to be.

Did I wrestle with the assignment? Yes! It would require something of me. It would challenge me and mature me. It would initially make me uncomfortable and uncertain, ever pushing me to rely on the Lord instead of myself.

Would God equip me? He did! I had already found great satisfaction and joy in teaching, but God stretched me beyond my past experience, equipping me all along the way to relationally teach university students.

Did the assignment eventually change? Yes, it did, but my primary purpose did not. Since my husband's death in 2005, God has moved me back into women's ministry. This assignment has expanded over the years to include writing as well as teaching and training internationally. But no matter where or how I teach, being *filled with the knowledge of His will* must always be my primary purpose. The essential key to knowing His will is abiding in Christ and allowing His Word to abide in me.

Are you searching for purpose? Are you asking the Lord for an assignment, a ministry, a relationship, or a job? Have you made it your life's goal to first seek and know God's heart? Moses needed purpose. He found it on the backside of the desert at the burning bush when he surrendered his life and his plans to the Almighty. Purpose is available for you as well. Surrender to Christ is the starting point. Abiding daily in Him is the life that follows. His plans for you will unfold in His time and in His way, bearing good fruit that always glorifies Him.

Discussion Questions
Desperate for Purpose

1. Moses has a dramatic encounter at Mt. Horeb when he first meets God (Exodus 3:1-10). Describe how this encounter changes his life. What changed in your life when you met Christ? Read 2 Corinthians 5:17 and Colossians 1:13-14

2. God's will—His purpose—is not about us. It is about Him and requires our surrender. What excuses does Moses give to God when God invites Moses to join His purpose? Can you relate to any of Moses' excuses?

3. Discuss the differences between these two questions: What is God's will for my life? and What is God's will?

4. Read again Paul's prayer in Colossians 1:9-11. What is Scripture teaching us about being filled with the knowledge of God's will? What does it mean to walk worthy? What does it mean to bear fruit?

5. God initiates our assignments. Looking back, what are some assignments God has given you? Every Christian has at least one spiritual gift given by the Holy Spirit for the work of service and building up the church (Ephesian 4: 12). Can you identify your spiritual gift(s)? Can you see how your assignments and your spiritual gifts work together in serving others?

6. Review the four principles that can help you seek God's direction in making decisions. Describe a personal experience when you used one of these principles to make an important decision? (Psalm 119:105, John 14:16-17, Proverbs 19:20, Romans 8:28)

3

DESPERATE
For Answers
Job 1-42

If anyone deserves to ask hard questions about suffering, it's Job. This ancient man who experiences incomprehensible loss asks sincere questions but gets very few answers from God. In fact, he gets none.

For most of us, unanswered questions about suffering create a tension within us, and because of that tension, I have hesitated to write this chapter. I can't offer tidy answers or perfect resolutions for Job's grief and pain. Truthfully, I want to turn away from his pain. It's too much, too deep to even attempt to understand, much less explain. My greatest hesitation in writing this chapter, however, is that I cannot offer *you* tidy answers and perfect resolutions for your pain and suffering. Likewise, there are no simple answers for my own.

The question of human suffering, especially the suffering of God's people, is a mystery. If we are not careful, the mystery of suffering in our own lives or in the lives of those we love will cause us to blame God and question His goodness. While it's difficult to understand in the crucible of suffering, the human experience, no matter how intense, is not the measure of truth. If we evaluate God through the lens of our own experiences, especially the painful ones, we will always have a diminished or distorted view of God.

God's Word is where we find a truthful estimation of God. His Word is the standard of measure—the truth that never changes even when our circumstances do. He has chosen to reveal Himself to us through His Word, and His supreme revelation is Jesus Christ. If you want a clear picture of God, look to Jesus. Even as you suffer, even as you grieve, even as you question, look to Jesus through the lens of God's Word. Like Job, when our focus is turned toward the Savior, we can worship even in the dust...even on the edge of desperate.

Job, the Man

The book of Job is considered one of the oldest books in the Bible. Much of the book is written in ancient poetic form. It is unique to the Old Testament because it is not about a nation, rather it is about God's dealings with a man named Job. Job's story has been the benchmark of human suffering for thousands of years. Volumes have been written about this difficult book. A casual reading of the book may cause us to cast Job as the central figure in the story, but on a deeper level, Job's story is God's story. However silent God may seem throughout a great portion of the book, make no mistake, God is central in the story of Job.

Job is introduced to us as a righteous man (Job 1:1). He is not a sinless man, but God has done a redemptive work in Job. God has chosen to have a relationship with Job, and Job has responded with reverence, obedience, and honor. His relationship with God affects every area of his life. Knowing and revering God enhances every relationship Job has and every endeavor he undertakes.

Job is blessed with ten children and perhaps grandchildren since it seems his seven sons and three daughters are adults. His family is his greatest blessing, and as a good father and priest of his family, Job watches over their spiritual condition with great care (Job 1:4-5).

Job is also a successful and wealthy businessman. To the modern reader, it seems he simply owns a lot of livestock, but each group of animals listed represents a business (Job 1:3). The sheep are a wool and meat business; the camels are a transportation business; the oxen are a farming business; the female donkeys are a symbol of power and wealth as well as the ancient transporter of goods from one place to another. He also has servants to oversee and work in each business. The man is industrious and wealthy, but more than that, Job is highly influential.

The pleasant introduction of Job covers only the first five verses of the book. By the end of Chapter Two, he has lost all ten children along with his enormous wealth and most of his servants. Finally, Job loses his health. He is given no forewarning, no solutions, and no insight as to why such horrific tragedies have come. His trauma eventually gives way to grieving questions answered by misinformed and shortsighted friends. While Job never curses God or renounces his Redeemer, he will question and misunderstand the ways of God.

This ancient book is not an easy read. It is difficult to grasp the severity of Job's suffering and *not* have questions about God. Admittedly, I have misunderstood the heart of God in seasons of suffering. Perhaps you have too. Certainly, our questions are not inconsequential to the Lord, but doubts and questions during seasons of suffering are often fueled by deep emotions. While emotions are ever present and God designed, they cannot be the rudder that guides us.

Truth must guide us. Like Job, we must learn to trust that God is completely sovereign, and in His sovereignty, He is perfectly wise and perfectly love. These are truths to store in our hearts long before suffering comes. Knowing and trusting God's sovereignty, wisdom, and love must become deep and daily waters, readily available in the dust of desperation.

God Is Sovereign

While the wealth of Job is staggering and the family of Job is admirable, it is the righteous character of Job that makes his story so alarming. After highlighting the great blessings of Job, Scripture shifts the narrative from righteous Job to a scene in heaven. Keep in mind as you read, Job has no knowledge of the heavenly scene or the conversation between God and Satan. In fact, Job will never know of it, but certainly his life will be altered by it.

Now there was a day when the sons of God came to present themselves before the LORD, and Satan also came among them. (Job 1:6)

For a season Satan has access to both heaven and earth. On this day, he comes into the presence of God along with other angels. Certainly, Satan is not there for a friendly visit. He hates God, and he hates anything and anyone that God loves. Every motivation, every action, and every thought of Satan is an attempt to wound and discredit God. Satan is the accuser, and on this day, he will accuse both God and Job. Make no mistake, Satan is not a free agent doing whatever he pleases. God is always sovereignly in control.

God is the first to speak, asking Satan where he has been. Satan replies he has been roaming the earth (Job 1:7). Shockingly, God asks Satan if he has taken notice of faithful, righteous, God-fearing Job. *Don't miss this!* God is the one who brings up Job's name. God is the one who shifts the conversation toward Job. God's question to Satan is not random or off-the-cuff. God has a plan. He knows what He is doing. Satan, however, defaults to his wicked nature and immediately begins to accuse.

Satan accuses God of playing favorites (Job 1:10), and he accuses Job of behaving righteously only to gain blessings from God (Job 1:9). To prove his point, Satan throws down a challenge. He challenges God to *"put forth Your hand now and touch (strike) all that he has; he will surely curse you to your face."* The challenge is not primarily about wounding Job. The challenge is about discrediting God.

The Enemy is trying to prove that Job is an unrighteous man; that it is only the great blessings of God that matter to Job, not his relationship with God. If Job curses God, it will make a mockery of God's redemptive work in Job. Furthermore, if Job renounces God, redemption will be called into question for all time. Going all the way back to Genesis 3:15 and God's declaration that Satan's head would be crushed by the seed of woman (Jesus), Satan has been on a ruthless quest to discredit, ruin, or annul God's plan of salvation. In Job's case, the Enemy wants to apply enough pain and pressure to cause God's redemptive work in Job to fall apart. He wants Job to curse God and walk away.

While Job's story may seem needlessly tragic to us, through it God is setting an indisputable standard; He is completely in control. God is sovereign over **all things**. His plan for the ages and, most definitely, for redemption will not be thwarted— not in Job's life and not in yours or mine. No matter the circumstances, the battles, the tragedies, or the Enemy's ploy— redemption stands. Sovereign grace cannot be annulled.

God allows Satan to carry out his diabolical challenge, but not because God has great confidence in Job. God allows the suffering because God has confidence in His own work of redemption. God's confidence is in His own authority and His own sovereign grace. He will not abandon His servant Job. He will not let go. He will see His work of redemption through, even if Job misunderstands and struggles in the process. God knows that in the struggle, Job will come through the fire of pain like gold—refined and reshaped to a deeper knowledge of God and a deeper trust in God.

This is good news for us. When God does a saving work in us through Jesus Christ, that work is eternal. It is sealed by the Holy Spirit (Ephesians 1:13). Nothing can undo what God has done. He began the good work of salvation in us, and He will see it to completion (Philippians 1:6). He will not let go of us even in the darkest storms and fiercest battles. God is confident in His own authority to save and redeem. He is completely in control. God may allow difficult things to come into our lives, not because He trusts our ability to hang on but because He trusts Christ in us. He has confidence in His redemptive work through His Son Jesus Christ.

While the end of God's conversations with Satan in Job 1:12 and Job 2:6-7 may not sound encouraging to us, both passages resonate with God's sovereign control.

Then the Lord said to Satan, "Behold all that he has is in your power, only do not put forth your hand on him." So Satan departed from the presence of God. (Job 1:12)

So the Lord said to Satan, "Behold, he is in your power, only spare his life." Then Satan went out from the presence of the Lord.... (Job 2:6-7)

Notice what God says and notice how Satan responds.

God gives Satan permission to touch all that Job has and later to touch Job's health. *Permission? Yes!* Satan cannot bring anything into the life of a believer unless it goes through the loving hands of God. Remember, Satan is not a free agent doing whatever he pleases. God is in control. While God gives Satan permission, God also sets the boundaries. In Chapter One, Satan is allowed to strike anything Job has, but he cannot touch Job. In Chapter Two, Satan is allowed to put his hand against Job, but Satan cannot take Job's life. Satan does not argue or negotiate with God about the boundaries. He can't. Even Satan submits to God's authority.

God's sovereignty saturates every page of Scripture. It is an inexhaustible characteristic of God. Yet in adversity, we often struggle with it. We either question His sovereignty or we question His goodness in exercising His sovereignty. As I have stated before, God does not lay aside one characteristic to display another.

J. I. Packer writes, "God's sovereignty, His constant care and absolute rule over all creation, is for His own glory and the good of His people. God never pursues His own glory at the expense of His people." Goodness and sovereignty are not a choice we have to make. He is both good and sovereign, even in the life of Job and even in our own suffering.

Who can speak and have it happen if the Lord has not decreed it? Is it not from the mouth of the Most High that both calamity and good things come? (Lamentations 3:37-38)

This passage from Lamentations is difficult to choke down, especially if we make God into our own image, if we imagine that He thinks and operates as we would. If we allow our perception of God to be limited by our own understanding, we will be sidetracked by doubts that can quickly turn to bitterness. Instead, God invites us to trust Him. The weeping prophet Jeremiah also writes in Lamentations 3:32, *"For if He causes grief, then He will have compassion according to His abundant lovingkindness."*

In seasons of suffering, it is a natural human inclination to ask questions or offer explanations. We all want answers to the pain and disappointments we experience, but God rarely, if ever, explains Himself to us. It is in the absence of explanations, however, we can find rest in the sovereignty of God. We will never be able to fully wrap our heads around His sovereignty, but we can trust Him. He is not capricious, fickle, or mean in His dealings with us. He is holy without a speck of wrongdoing in Him. Even if agents of evil are working through people or circumstances, God is still in control.

Certainly, there are mysteries we will never understand

on this side of Heaven, but we can confidently trust His Word and His perfect character. Trusting God always honors God. Trusting Him is also where we experience rest, comfort, and hope.

"My thoughts are not your thoughts, and your ways are not My ways," declares the Lord. "For as the heavens are higher than the earth, so are My ways higher than your ways, and My thoughts than your thoughts." (Isaiah 55:8-9)

For the Lord of hosts has planned, and who can frustrate it? And as for His stretched-out hand, who can turn it back? (Isaiah 14:27)

For me, I have never been given clear explanations for the tragic accident that took my husband's life or for the suffering and confusion that followed my family for years. Likewise, there has never been a solid response to my heartbroken *why.* But this I know—God is completely, sovereignly in control of all things. I have also learned (and still learning) that His sovereignty is a place of comfort and rest when life is perplexing. While I will never understand the ways of God, I can trust Him. Nothing will snatch me from His hands. Furthermore, His redeeming work cannot be undone by any circumstance or event. Not in my life. Not in yours.

God Is Wise

God never makes a mistake. He knows what He is doing. He sees the beginning and end of creation and time. His sovereign plan for the ages and for our lives is never up for discussion. God never agonizes over any decision. Why? Because His wisdom is infinite and infallible; everything God does is perfect.

Jerry Bridges defines wisdom as "good judgment, the best response to a given situation, the ability to develop the best course of action, discernment" (*Trusting God*, 118). God's course of action is always perfect because His wisdom is perfect.

Job's friends had little understanding of God's wisdom. To them, Job's ordeal is God's reaction to some secret sin in Job's life or in the lives of his children. His friends can't fathom that everything taking place in Job's life is covered in God's perfect wisdom. These misinformed friends had a narrow "cause and effect" theology. Some theologians call it a retribution theology. Their logic assumes bad things happen because we are bad and good things happen because we are good. Read the words of Eliphaz, Job's friend.

Remember now, whoever perished being innocent? Or where were the upright destroyed? According to what I have seen, those who plow iniquity and those who sow trouble harvest it. By the breath of God they perish, and by the blast of His nostrils they come to an end. (Job 4:7-9)

Job's friends understand that God is Almighty, but they wrongly view a relationship with God as a business contract: God will do His part when we do ours, and if we don't do our part, there will be retribution. Today, there are subtle twists to this false dogma that many Christians have embraced. Some assume there is an automatic connection between material and physical prosperity and one's spirituality. Others deduce that we must perform well, keeping all the rules and living perfectly, or else God will punish us with calamity. However, both erroneous views put man at the center of things and not God—and not His perfect wisdom.

God has always dealt with His people in perfect wisdom. He is not a vengeful God, hurling retribution when we step out of line. Relationship with God has always been based on God's grace, not our behavior (Deuteronomy 7:7-8, Ephesians 2:8-9). Obedience has always been the humble and loving response God desires (Deuteronomy 7:9, Romans 12:1).

False teachings about earthly blessings subtly infer we can manipulate God. In fact, it's the very thing Satan accuses Job of doing, behaving favorably toward God to insure His blessings. Yes, there is great blessing in loving and serving God, but God is not obligated to any of us. God extinguishes any question of His obligation to Job or to us when He asks, *"Who has given to Me that I should repay him?"* (Job 41:11)

Sadly, we often miss the truth that our greatest blessings are not material or physical blessings at all; rather, they are spiritual blessings that are ours in Christ (Ephesians 1:3-14). We cannot twist God's arm to give us more than He has already given us in Christ. We cannot demand God pour out rigorous health, earthly wealth, and physical protection because we are His children. God has already given us everything we need for life and godliness through Christ (2 Peter 1:3). There is no bank account, no mansion, no clean bill of health, no unscathed life that can match our glorious riches in Christ Jesus. To demand such things in our theology is to diminish what is already ours. Likewise, no amount of rule keeping can elicit more from His hands. We cannot add penitence, rituals, works, or religion to the already perfect work of redemption by grace through faith (Ephesians 2:8-9, Galatians 3:2-3).

95

Furthermore, we are not to live in fear that retribution is just one misstep away. God is not vengeful, zapping His people with hardship when they step out of line. Any attempt to ward off God's judgment by keeping rules or following religion will always lead to unnecessary fear. Christ has paid the price for our sin. There is no condemnation for those who are in Christ (Romans 8:1). Certainly the Lord will discipline and correct us when needed, but He is not responding to us with retribution. Job's friends have it all wrong.

For me, the thing that makes the Book of Job so difficult is that his three friends and then a fourth onlooker speak nuggets of truth about God here and there, but they always misapply that truth. They constantly revert to faulty thinking, assuming the problem with Job is Job. Their wisdom is limited. Their perception of God is short-sighted. Their theology is guided by human logic and not truth. If we are not careful, we will do the same thing.

My late husband's mother died of breast cancer five months after Dana and I married. In her final months of life, a few of her friends came to visit and pray with her. Unfortunately, her friends would have served her better if they had stayed away. They espoused the same false doctrine that plagued Job's friends. Those misinformed women told my suffering mother-in-law there was some secret sin she had not confessed or perhaps something in her past for which she had not repented, otherwise God would have already healed her cancer. My blood still boils a little at the thought of their careless words.

My precious mother-in-law was a godly woman who loved the Lord and served Him throughout her life, even though much of her life was difficult. She knew the truth of God's Word, but in her pain the seeds of doubt planted by those women nagged at her. Through many late-night conversations with my husband, her son, God's peace overcame the lies. In great physical pain, she died trusting her Redeemer—a testimony of faith to all of us who had watched her journey.

Listen carefully. God operates in the world, in history, in people, in circumstances, and most assuredly, in the lives of His children based on His sovereign authority—not a business contract. And His sovereignty is always exercised with perfect wisdom. His wisdom sees the beginning and the end. His wisdom cannot be measured or understood by our limited minds. His wisdom undergirds every decision He makes, and He never makes a mistake. His wisdom is never exercised apart from His love.

Evelyn Underhill said, "If God were small enough to be understood He would not be big enough to be worshipped" (qtd in *Secure in the Everlasting Arms,* 91). We cannot whittle God down to our understanding and still rest in His wisdom and His ways. In our limited way of thinking and operating, we would alleviate all suffering. We would fix things so that pain is never a part of life's equation. Yet, God uses our pain to accomplish what only He can accomplish through it. In perfect wisdom He works for our good, and our greatest good is to know Him more intimately. Elizabeth Elliot wrote,

The deepest things that I have learned in my own life have come from the deepest suffering. And out of the deepest waters and the hottest fires have come the deepest things I know about God" (*Suffering is Never for Nothing,* 9).

After a speaking engagement several years ago, I met with a young widow. She and her husband were married only six months when they were involved in a car accident. He was killed. She suffered life-altering injuries. Her brokenhearted words to me still resonate in my mind as I write this chapter. She said, "Jennifer, people tell me I am going to learn so much through this terrible tragedy. But am I so stupid that this is what God has to use to teach me?" I cried with her and prayed with her...and pondered her question long after that evening. Job's ordeal, and even my own loss, has helped me embrace the mystery of God's ways when there are no comfortable answers.

God is not slinging fiery ordeals at us to teach us great lessons; neither is He punishing us for some secret sin. But in the fire and in the waters that come, God reveals Himself to us in ways we could have never known without the pain. God is wise, dear one. Job's friends misunderstood God and the depth of God's wisdom. Job doubted and misunderstood too. Hurting hearts almost always do.

Before the hurt invades, we can learn to value and trust His wisdom as we daily spend time in God's Word and in prayerful conversation with Him. The Holy Spirit daily builds a firm foundation of truth in our lives that no flood or fire can destroy—even if for a season we wrestle. We will be reminded in both sunshine and shadow that He never makes a mistake. He has an eternal perspective while our perspective is limited. Yet even in our limited perspective, we can trust His matchless wisdom because it flows from His perfect, faithful, unchangeable nature.

God is sovereign. God is wise. And, oh, to grasp the depths of it.... God is love.

God Is Love

While many of us have been taught since birth that God is love, it is often the first characteristic of God called into question when suffering invades. Perhaps it is because while sovereignty and wisdom are lofty and magnificent, love is personal. It's His love for us that brings salvation, forgives our sin, and buoys us in trials. Yet of all the wonderful, matchless characteristics of God, it is His love we most often fashion into our own image. We want God to love as we would love, and when He doesn't—we struggle.

The ancient Greek language has many words for love, but when the New Testament refers to God's love, the word *agape* is always used to describe God's love for humanity. We have come to define *agape* as unconditional love, yet it is richer and deeper than any simplistic definition. Indeed, God's love is unconditional in that we cannot earn it, we do not deserve it, and our behavior cannot thwart it. God's love is not something He dispenses or contains—God is love itself. His very nature is love. He never lays aside His love only to pick it up later. *Agape* is who God is (1 John 4:8).

God's love is a love of the will. His love is not a feeling or sentiment that vacillates with circumstances or our behavior. He loves us the way we need to be loved rather than the way we want to be loved. The truth of God's love is something we must store in our hearts long before trials come. If our understanding of His love is incomplete or shallow, we will view God through the blurred lens of our circumstances instead of through the perfectly focused lens of His willful love.

Remember in Chapter One of this book we discussed Mary, Martha, and Lazarus? Remember John 11:5? Scripture emphasizes Jesus' love for all three of these dear friends, and yet the alarming chain of events that follow seems to dispute His love for them. Mary and Martha certainly felt like Jesus' initial lack of action fell short of His love for them. We often feel the same way.

Our perspective about love is almost always linked to happiness or blissful circumstances. We want God to love like we would love. If it were up to us, we would fix the problem, relieve the suffering, change the circumstances, grant the request, and we would do it on our terms, with our wisdom, and in our time. Disappointment with God is sure to come when we expect God to operate within our finite purview of love. Dear one, God IS love. He can be nothing less even if suffering and trials remain.

Reading the book of Job thousands of years after it was written can make us a little harsh in our judgment of Job and his friends. They all seem to have limited and misinformed ideas about God and His ways. Keep in mind Job and his friends probably lived around the same time as Abraham. They were not alive when God chose Israel and gave the Mosaic Law. Their understanding of God was limited to the revelation God had given about Himself *at that time*. Additionally, they had no knowledge of the New Covenant and certainly could not fathom salvation through Jesus Christ, who is God incarnate. Consequently, they had little understanding of God's love. To them, He was the Almighty, Creator, just, and righteous…but love seems to be a minor, if not foreign, idea to all of them.

Interestingly, the relational name of Yahweh (LORD) is only found in the first two chapters of Job and again in the final chapters when God is speaking (Job 38-42). Relationship with God with love as the cornerstone is not prevalent in their theology. So while the attitude of Job's friends (and sometimes even Job) is unsettling, we can sympathize with their lack of understanding. You and I, however, have much more available to us than these ancient men ever had.

As Christians, we have God living within us through the Holy Spirit, and we have God's complete revelation of truth in Jesus Christ and His Word, the Bible. There is no new truth for God to impart, but for us there is a lifetime of learning all that He has revealed in Christ and in His Word. The Holy Spirit is our teacher, always using God's Word to guide us into truth (John 14:26, 16:13).

We know God is love because God's love permeates His Word. We know God is love because God's love is perfectly demonstrated in Jesus Christ. We know God is love because *God so loved the world that He gave His only begotten Son, that whoever believes in Him should not perish, but have eternal life* (John 3:16).

We have every opportunity to know and experience the perfect love of God daily and intimately through Christ. We are invited to drink deeply from His well of love. We are admonished to sink our roots into the soil of His Word and allow truth to anchor us, especially the truth of His love. Love—agape—never fails, never runs out on us, never comes up short, never lets go. *God is love, dear one*. Bury that truth deep in your soul and be assured of it when desperation robs you of sentimentality and good feelings.

But God demonstrated His own love toward us, in that while we were yet sinners, Christ died for us. (Romans 5:8)

For I am convinced that neither death, nor life, nor angels, nor principalities, nor things present, nor things to come, nor powers, nor height, nor depth, nor any other created thing, shall be able to separate us from the love of God, which is in Christ Jesus our Lord. (Romans 8:38-39)

See how great a love the Father has bestowed upon us, that we should be called children of God, and such we are. (1 John 3:1

And this is love, not that we loved God, but that He loved us and sent His son.... (1 John 4:10)

But God, being rich in mercy, because of His great love with which He has loved us, even when we were dead in our transgressions, made us alive together with Christ (by grace you have been saved) .... (Ephesians 2:4-5)

I have loved you with an everlasting love; therefore I have drawn you with lovingkindness. (Jeremiah 31:3)

But You, Lord, are a compassionate and gracious God, slow to anger and abounding in faithful love and truth. (Psalm 86:15 CSB)

A final thought in this brief section on God's infinite love: God's love for us is not an excuse for careless living. We cannot take lightly the great cost of God's love demonstrated to us in Christ. Instead, God's love constrains us to trust Him completely and live for Him wholly. Job had limited knowledge of God's love, but we don't. It has been revealed to the fullest in Jesus Christ.

God is sovereign, God is wise, and God is love. Let these truths beat like a drum in your heart. Never quieted. Never extinguished. Never doubted. Even on the edge of desperate.

Our Response

This chapter is not intended to be an expositional study of the book of Job. It is an attempt to examine the great suffering of Job in hopes that we will find strength and comfort in our own times of suffering. While Job does not respond perfectly in every situation, he experiences God's desired outcome in the end. Job responds to his suffering with grief, questions, worship, and, finally, surrender. Surrender is God's desired outcome for us as well when we walk through difficulty, but He also knows we will grieve and question in the process.

We grieve. Looking back at the first chapter of Job, we have already discussed that God gave Satan permission to touch all that Job had. It is painful to read what Satan did, described to the reader in rapid succession.

- The Sabeans, an ancient people from Sheba, attack and steel Job's donkeys and oxen—wiping out two of Job's lucrative businesses. The Sabeans murder Job's servants (employees) who were caring for the livestock. Only one servant escapes to tell Job about the disaster (Job 1:13-15).
- Fire falls from heaven and burns up the sheep as well as the servants caring for the sheep—another business is destroyed, and faithful workers killed. Only one servant escapes to tell Job of the great loss (Job 1:16).
- The group of Chaldeans, an ethnic group in Job's country, formed three marauding bands who steel Job's camels and murder the servants caring for them. Only one servant escapes to deliver the bad news to Job. Job's fourth business and his last remaining wealth is obliterated. Except for the three messengers, all his

employees are wiped out as well (Job 1:17). But the worst is yet to come.

- All ten of Job's children, and presumably their spouses and children, are feasting together at the oldest brother's house. A wind comes across the wilderness and causes the roof of the house to collapse, killing everyone. Only one servant escapes to tell of the horrors   (Job 1:18-19).

How does Job respond? *He grieves.* True to his culture, his cries of anguish are accompanied by tearing his robe, shaving his head, and falling on his face in the dust. Job holds nothing back as he expresses physically what words cannot adequately capture. There are no gentle tears, instead there is gut-wrenching anguish spilling over in every way.

If Chapter One isn't sobering enough, Chapter Two intensifies Job's sorrow with acute physical pain. When Job's three friends see Job, he is unrecognizable, sitting in a heap of ashes, scraping infected sores with a piece of broken pottery (Job 2:7-13). The silence that ensues for seven days is indicative of the deep depression that has overtaken Job. Grief has settled into every bone and into every thought of God's righteous servant Job.

As Job grieves, Mrs. Job has a few thoughts of her own. Remember, she has lost greatly too. All ten of her children, possibly her grandchildren, her lifestyle, and finally her husband's ability to care for her have all been lost. Mrs. Job takes a different approach to sorrow than her husband. She turns away from God. She spits words of bitterness at Job, mocking his integrity and chiding him to curse God and die. Interestingly, these are the very things Satan wants Job to do. Job, however, turns toward God—even as he grieves.

In 1969 in her book *On Death and Dying*, psychiatrist Elisabeth Kubler-Ross introduced the theory that grief is divided into five stages: anger, denial, bargaining, depression, and acceptance. Much has been written about her theory, and most mental health experts adhere to her conclusions. But long before modern psychiatry weighed in on the matter of grief, Scripture, especially the Psalms, has given us poignant examples of grieving—grieving that turns us toward God.

Following the story of Job into Chapter Three, Job does not curse God or reject God, but he does pour out a dark response aimed at God's ears. In his pain and sorrow, Job curses the day he was born. He wonders aloud why he is still alive. He longs for death. He asks mournful but unanswerable questions. He says God is the one who has hedged him in. Job Chapter Three is a lament: a verbal, passionate complaint expressing confusion, pain, and hurt.

The Psalms are filled with laments. They are prayers directed squarely at God, but filled with questions, sorrow, and disappointment. At times the psalmist may seem irreverent because his grief speaks with great emotion. Yet, the grieving expressions of the psalmist are the first steps toward healing and transformation.

How long, O LORD? Will you forget me forever? How long will you hide your face from me? How long must I take counsel in my soul and have sorrow in my heart all the day? How long shall my enemy be exalted over me? (Psalm 13:1-2 ESV)

My tears have been my food day and night, while they say to me all day long, "Where is your God?" .... O my God, my soul is in despair within me.... I will say to God, my rock, "Why hast Thou forgotten me?" ...(Psalm 42:3,6,9 NASV)

Will the Lord reject forever? And will He never be favorable again? Has His lovingkindness ceased forever? Has His promise come to an end forever? Has God forgotten to be gracious? Or has He in anger withdrawn His compassion? (Psalm 77:7-9 NASV)

Job grieved. The psalmist grieved. Even Jesus grieved in the Garden of Gethsemane and on the cross (Luke 22:41-44, Matthew 27:46). They all express their deep ache through lament. They pour out anguish—but they pour it out to God.

I believe the Bible encourages us to grieve; even more, it encourages us to lament: to put words to our pain and speak them out loud to God. The Lord already knows our thoughts. He knows our sorrow. To honestly speak what we are feeling, to wrestle out loud, is not a form of doubting God; rather, it is entrusting our deepest hurts to the One who cares the most about us.

My friend D. Ray Davis has written extensively about grief since losing his wife unexpectedly. He encourages Christians to voice their own lament when pain, sorrow, or grief are overwhelming, even though initially it may feel uncomfortable complaining to God. Lamenting, he writes, is a Biblical way to face the hurt. It is where healing begins. But most importantly, lamenting is freeing. Read what my friend wrote about his own journey of lament.

Honestly, complaining seemed very uncomfortable to me. It seemed disrespectful. However, I could not deny it was biblical.

David and other writers complained. Even Jesus lamented in Matthew 27:46, "My God, my God, why have you forsaken me?" And Jesus was quoting Psalm 22.

So, I complained. Uncomfortable, yes. But I sought to complain respectfully. Carefully.

And something beautiful happened. Jesus spoke to my heart and helped me see I was right to complain. This brokenness was not God's design. However, brokenness is real. But he whispered to my heart that brokenness was worse than I could even fathom. Beyond my singular loss, the whole world is broken. And then it was as if he leaned in and delivered the news that brokenness is so bad that it cost him his life on the cross. (facinglossblog.com, December 5, 2022)

The Apostle Paul encourages us to grieve as people with hope (1 Thessalonians 4:13). Listen carefully. Our hope is not in good circumstances. Our hope is not that God will restore all that has been lost. Our hope is not in human resolutions to our problems. Our hope is in Christ. Christ died to redeem the brokenness of sin and the brokenness of a fallen world. He may not restore all that sin, sickness, and suffering has taken from us, but He redeems. Because of the cross, He buys back our sorrows and makes them into something new that glorifies Him. He gives hope that our suffering is only for a season, that heaven is real, and that life in Christ, here and now, is meaningful. In his book *Dark Clouds and Deep Mercy*, Mark Vroegop writes, "Lament is the language of the people who know the whole story—the Gospel story."

Dear reader, if in your grief, any voice tells you that God has forgotten to love you or He has abandoned you or He is not sovereign or He does not work in perfect wisdom—rest assured...those voices are wrong. We have hope! God will finish the good work of salvation He has started in you. In your suffering and sorrow, grieve hard and lament truthfully, always turning toward your loving Heavenly Father who has given us hope in Christ.

We question. Job has often been described as patient. Likewise, patient people are sometimes described as having "the patience of Job." But reading the entire account of Job, we see that his patience wears thin for much of the book. He persistently asks questions about his suffering, and his most often repeated question is *why*.

How long will You not look away from me, nor leave me alone till I swallow my spit? If I sin, what do I do to You, You watcher of mankind? Why have You made me Your mark? Why have I become a burden to You? (Job 7:19-20 ESV)

I will say to God, "Do not condemn me; let me know why you contend with me." (Job 10:2 NASV)

Why do You hide Your face and count me as Your enemy? (Job 13:24ESV)

While these questions don't sound like a patient man, they certainly portray a suffering and even confused man. Everything he knows and thinks about God is being questioned, and Job directs those questions to God. It may seem to us that some of Job's questions border on irreverence, but his questions are also punctuated with great statements of faith (Job 13:15, 19:25). His grief and faith are mingled with confusion; consequently, heavy-hearted questions spill out, bringing the point to us: Is it okay to question God?

Scripture tells us yes—but with boundaries.

We have already looked at several psalms of lament, each of them freely asking questions to God. But let's focus our attention briefly on David. His psalms of lament give us further insight into questioning God during times of suffering.

David, the shepherd, the king, and the psalmist, is referred to as a man after God's own heart (1 Samuel 13:14). Yet in times of great sorrow and confusion, David questions God (Psalm 6,13,22 and 142 are good examples). So, how can a man after God's own heart question God? Shouldn't David's faith have been perfectly exercised and expressed even in trials? God's glowing description of David and David's questions to God seem to be a contradiction. In fact, they aren't.

David's relationship with God is the centerpiece of his life. In sorrow, David turns toward God. In suffering, he turns toward God. In confusion and fear, David seeks God. In sin, he repents to God. Everything about David's imperfect life ultimately centers on God. For David to raise heartbroken questions to God is not an act of doubt or defiance; neither is it a contradiction of God's description of him. David's questions are an act of trust. David understands that life is not a series of chance happenings. God holds all the answers. And God holds David. And Job. And us.

God invites our questions, and He responds with mercy. Our parameters are to ask with a God-centered heart instead of an upraised fist. We cannot demand answers from God, but we can come boldly to His throne of grace and find help and mercy in times of great need (Hebrews 4:16). Coming boldly may entail bringing questions, but we bring them being ever mindful it is HIS throne, and HE is God.

Years ago, a dear family member lost his wife after her long and agonizing battle with cancer. After her death, my family member railed at God. He didn't just ask God broken-hearted questions; he accused God with unrelenting anger. My dear family member died with his resentment toward God fully intact. While I cannot attest to the eternal condition of his soul, I can tell you the quality of his earthly life diminished greatly because of bitterness towards God.

God is never obligated to explain Himself. When we pose questions to God, demands have no place. If God chooses to be silent on the subject or if He gives no clear answers to our questions, our response is faith…trusting Him regardless. God may not give the answers we desire, but He always gives Himself. And oh, precious reader, He is enough.

God's silence throughout most of Job's story is unsettling. In our estimation, God should have spoken up long before Chapter Thirty-Eight. If only He had let Job in on the cosmic conversation between God and Satan, at least Job could have had some solace, some understanding in the trials. But God is silent. And Job grieves. And Job questions.

Job's story is not a one-dimensional story. God is doing more than Job could imagine. Yes, God is doing a transformational work in Job, but God is also at work for an eternal purpose in generations yet to be born. Remember, God's redemption has been challenged by Satan, and while Job is the one who suffers, we are the beneficiaries of his trials. Job's story is a marker in time, reminding us that redemption stands. God is faithful. He can be trusted. No one and nothing can snatch us from His hands or separate us from His love. Job is a testimony to God's secure grace.

Likewise, our stories are not one-dimensional stories. God is doing more than we could ever imagine through the trials and sorrows of our lives. Yes, He is doing a transformational work in us, but He is also doing an eternal and generational work in us. As our children, our families, our neighbors, and our churches watch our struggles, we can become living testimonies of God's sovereignty, wisdom, and love. In our frailty, God is glorified, He does not let go, He works with purpose and care…and nothing can negate God's redemption. God can be trusted.

So after the needed grieving and the humble questioning, how do we respond to God in times of suffering? The same way Job initially responds. We worship.

We worship. Job had been a worshipping man for much of his life. As the priest of his home, he regularly offered sacrifices to God on behalf of himself and his family. The New Testament speaks of being a living sacrifice (Romans 12:1), and Job seems to have that mindset as he lives to honor God in all things. Job worshipped long before tragedy struck. In fact, worship was such an important part of Job's life, it seems to be a natural response when the first wave of tragedies rolls in.

Then Job arose and tore his robe and shaved his head, and he fell to the ground and worshipped. And he said, "Naked I came from my mother's womb, and naked I shall return there. The LORD gave and the LORD has taken away. Blessed be the name of the LORD." (Job 1:20-21)

Because worship is a natural part of his life, Job is able to worship through his tears. In the beginning, he has confidence in God even though he has no understanding of why God has allowed such suffering. While this is the only reference to worship in the entire book, it's good for us to recognize that Job's first response to suffering is worship. For us, grieving is necessary and questions have value, but worship is imperative in times of suffering.

Worship takes our eyes off of ourselves. It refocuses our attention on the Lord. It guards us from bitterness. It reminds us of who Christ is and all that He has done for us. Worship humbles us. It brings to mind our dependence on God's grace. Just as truth must be established in our minds before pain enters our lives, worship must be established before as well.

Again, the psalms of lament are good teachers. Every psalm of lament has a turning point. The grief and questions which the psalmist raise toward God are the very things that guide him to worship. Keep in mind, worship may or may not be a formal act. Worship is an attitude of the heart that can be expressed in a formal act, but most often worship is expressed daily as a humble, obedient, trusting life.

Job worships after the first round of trauma, but when the second wave of sorrow hits, Job's worship is, at best, vague. As the story progresses, Job is not simply a humbled man; he is a stripped man. Everything of value and everything that gives a man identity has been stripped away. After Job 1:20, we don't read of any other overt or formal acts of worship. But if we look closely at his words, Job's worshiping heart still flickers because God's sovereign grace remains steadfast.

Though He slay me, I will hope in Him. (Job 13:15)

And as for me, I know that my Redeemer lives, and at the last He will take His stand on the earth. Even after my skin is

destroyed, yet from my flesh I shall see God: whom I myself
shall behold, and whom my eyes shall see and not another. (Job
19:25-27)

But He knows the way I take; when He has tried me, I shall
come forth as gold....I have treasured the words of His mouth
more than my necessary food. It is God who has made my heart
faint, and the Almighty who has dismayed me, but I am not
silenced by the darkness nor the deep gloom which covers me.
(Job 23:10, 12, 16-17)

Job's worship of God may not entail confidently raised
hands or full-throated singing. It doesn't have the ring of
triumph, but he worships—in the dust, through the tears, and
sometimes only with a frail and fleeting whimper. Worship
has been cemented into Job's soul long before the devastating
trials. It surfaces, albeit rough and ragged, like a war-torn flag
still waving in the fiercest battle. Make no mistake. It is the
focus of worship, not the strength of the person, that matters.

One Sunday morning not long after my first husband
died, my sons and I visited a large church. While this church
was a dynamic church, it wasn't a highly expressive church.
As a rule, few people raised their hands or spontaneously
stood during the music. Neither were there random shouts of
affirmation during the preaching nor emotional movements
toward the altar. It was a Biblically sound but reserved
congregation.

On this particular Sunday, the three of us with ragged faith
and deep wounds sat quietly in the middle section of the huge
auditorium. We were surrounded by hundreds of people. The
service progressed at a typical pace, but the choir, a massive

113

throng of talented singers, was my undoing that morning. They sang a song directly from Psalm 3, *"Thou O LORD are a shield for me, my glory and the lifter of my head."* In my fresh grief, the words pierced me. With tears streaming down my face, I spontaneously stood to my feet with both hands raised high in broken abandonment to the Lord. I still remember it as a profound experience. I also remember I was the only person standing.

When the boys and I got into the car after the service, I sensed that my emotional and outward display of worship had embarrassed them. I tried to explain. "Guys, when Jesus is the only thing holding you together, you worship differently."

It's still true. Broken people pray differently and worship differently and live differently. Desperation compels us to lean harder on our Savior than we ever thought possible. In our brokenness, even in our heartbroken worship, His love draws us to surrender.

We surrender. Surrender is not defeat. For the Christian, it is the ultimate place of victory. Surrender is coming to the end of ourselves. It is abandoning our will to the will of Christ. Surrender is the willingness to accept anything God offers, even suffering. Surrender is a place of complete trust in the faithfulness of God, and it is a daily act of worship.

God finally speaks to Job in the closing chapters of the book. But it is important to note what God does NOT say.

- God never tells Job about the conversation with Satan. The reader knows, but Job never does.
- God does not answer any of Job's questions.
- God does not apologize for the suffering, nor does He explain it.

- God never mentions or acknowledges Job's trials.

Instead of explaining and answering Job's questions , God is the one asking questions of Job.

Where were you when I laid the foundation of the earth? Tell Me, if you have understanding. (Job 38:4)

Have you ever in your life commanded the morning and caused the dawn to know its place? (Job 38:12)

Is it by your understanding that the hawk soars, stretching his wings toward the south? Is it at your command that the eagle mounts up and makes his nest on high? (Job 39:26-27)

God speaks directly to Job about His power, majesty, and sovereignty using His creation to illustrate His words. God has put Job on trial, asking rapid and succinct rhetorical questions. At times, Job has been guilty of blaming God and asserting his own righteousness, declaring he does not deserve what God has dished out. God's probing questions quickly turn Job's heart to repentance.

Will the faultfinder contend with the Almighty? Let him who reproves God answer it. (Job 40:2)

Will you condemn Me that you may be justified? (Job 40:8)

Then Job answered the LORD and said, "Behold I am insignificant; what can I reply to Thee? I lay my hand on my mouth. (Job 40:3-4)

When God finishes His powerful discourse, Job's perspective and his heart have changed. Job knows God more intimately and trusts Him fully. Job abandons all of his questions and presuppositions. Pain and adversity have purified and matured Job's faith. In response, Job humbly bows in surrender (Job 42:2-6).

"I have heard of You by the hearing of my ear, but now my eye sees You." (Job 42:5)

The conclusion of Job's story can be problematic for some of us. God calls Job His servant; Job forgives his friends; then God not only restores Job's fortune but also doubles it. Beyond that, God gives Job ten more children and a long, full life. As you read, be careful of your conclusions. I used to have a problem with the ending. To me, it seemed as if God is trying to make things up to Job or that Job's surrender earned him great blessings. I felt like the book was giving us a tidy ribbon wrapped around a horrific ordeal like a "happily ever after" fairytale. Nothing could be further from the truth.

The ending is in keeping with the entire story. God is sovereign, wise, and, yes, love. He can do whatever He chooses to do. He can bring sorrow, or He can bring pleasure, but whatever He brings into our lives is for His glory and for His purpose. It isn't the material or physical blessings that keep our hearts bound to God. It is His grace. His redeeming work in us cannot be undone by painful circumstances nor enhanced by earthly blessings. Christ is enough. If thorns remain, if sickness rages, if finances falter, if relationships dissolve, the Lord remains faithful and worthy of our worship and our surrender.

On the other hand, if earthly riches increase, families flourish, and influence spreads, we must recognize quickly that none of these can surpass the blessing of knowing Christ.

While many Christians believe suffering should be the exception and not the rule, Scripture tells us that sin, shame, and suffering entered this world altogether when Adam and Eve sinned—when they found Satan more reliable than God. God's perfect creation was soiled, suffering became the rule, and nothing would be exempt from the effects of sin. But God redeems. His grace makes a way for salvation.

I end this chapter as I began it with no tidy answers for personal pain, especially in the life of a believer. Regardless of my lack of answers, I can point you to Christ. I can assure you there is purpose in the pain even if there are no explanations. For me, there have been no easy answers for the death of my husband, the pain of cancer, the sorrow over prodigals, or the challenges of remarriage. However, I can look back and confidently tell you—Christ has been enough. He always will be.

Precious reader, God is sovereign—trust Him. God is wise—lean into Him. God is love—love Him back. Bring your tears and your questions to His throne of grace and worship there. Surrender to the Redeemer who will never leave you nor forsake you.

Discussion Questions
Desperate for Answers

1. What are Satan's accusations against Job and against God? (Job 1:9-11) Even though God allows Satan to touch Job, God sets the boundaries and Satan does not question the boundaries. How does this encourage us when we feel pressed or persecuted? When life feels crushing?

2. Read Isaiah 55:8-9 and 11, Revelations 1:17-18. How does God's sovereignty hold us steady during difficult times? Does God's sovereignty help us come to terms with difficult questions, even if we never get answers or explanations?

3. Read 2 Peter 1:3 and Ephesians 1:3. When going through a serious physical need, an urgent financial concern, a family crisis, or a job challenge, are God's richest blessings still available to us? Is His wisdom always available to us? Read James 1:5.

4. Does God allow trials in our lives simply to teach us lessons? What does He reveal to us about Himself during trials? What has He revealed about Himself to you during difficult times?(Job 12:22)

5. Why is it important to store God's love in our hearts before the trials come? How does Romans 8:38-39 confirm His love? Are there passages of Scripture that are deeply meaningful in difficult times?

4

DESPERATE
For Truth
2 Kings 22-23

We live in an ever-changing world. Society changes.
Opinions shift. Standards are altered. Truth seems to be fluid
and subjective. Even in my own family, I notice differences
in opinions and standards among my five adult children.
Thirteen years separate our oldest child from the youngest, and
somehow in the thirteen-year span, a shift in ideology has taken
place. The youngest children think and respond very differently
to the world around them than the older children do.

While the differences in my adult children are sometimes
perplexing to me, the pattern is not new. Change is all around
us, and often our thinking and our behavior conform to societal
shifts. But where is the truth amid all the change? What is the

121

standard of measure for truth? Is it possible that truth for one person is different for another person—that we all operate in our own truth?

These are not new questions or new struggles. All of Scripture presents man's struggle with truth. At the very beginning in the Garden of Eden, Adam and Eve chose a lie over truth… a decision that has marred every person and all of creation from that time forward. Fast forward in Scripture to the Book of Judges. God's people chose to do what was *right in their own eyes*. They followed their own truth, which always led to a life of bondage and confusion. In the New Testament when questioning Jesus, Pontius Pilate asks the forlorn question, *"What is truth?"* (John 18:38). It seems people today are asking the same question and coming up short on definitive answers. For all of us, past and present, the problem with doing what is *right in our own eyes* or following our own truth is that the standard is inconsistent. The lines constantly move. What was touted as truth yesterday becomes negotiable today.

God, however, has given the standard of truth. His revealed Word, the Bible, is truth. All opinions, standards, social constructs, and ideology must be laid beside the straight edge of Scripture. If anything does not line up with God's Word, it is not truth, no matter how sincerely we may believe it to be true.

God's Word flows from His unchangeable faithful character; therefore, His Word is unchangeable and faithful. It never vacillates with time or circumstances, yet it is always relevant. It is not a rule book for us to occasionally reference. It is God's living and active Word—truth to live by and truth that transforms.

While Scripture was penned by some forty different writers, each with a distinct personality and purpose for writing, every word written is breathed or inspired by the Holy Spirit. Because God's Word is God-breathed, it is infallible and authoritative. Furthermore, God has sovereignly preserved it through the ages, giving it to us with His perfect heart of love.

The grass withers, the flower fades, but the word of our God stands forever. (Isaiah 40:8)

All Scripture is inspired by God and profitable for teaching, for reproof, for correction, for training in righteousness.... (2 Timothy 3:16)

The words of the LORD are pure words; as silver tried in a furnace on the earth, refined seven times. (Psalm 12:6)

For the word of God is alive and powerful. It is sharper than the sharpest two-edged sword, cutting between soul and spirit, between joint and marrow. It exposes our innermost thoughts and desires. (Hebrews 4:12 NLT)

People of Truth

Scripture is given to us by God. We cannot create authentic truth in our own minds. Contrary to modern society, which believes an individual can craft his own truth, Scripture tells us God reveals truth through His Word, and we can receive it. American author and theologian Paul David Tripp writes, "The authority of Scripture, that it is to be believed and obeyed, does not depend on the testimony of any one person, but completely on God, the author. It is to be joyfully received because it is the Word of God" (*Do You Believe*, 32).

You and I can know God because He reveals Himself to us. Certainly, He has clearly revealed Himself to us in His Word, but He has also revealed Himself to us through Jesus Christ. Jesus is the embodiment of truth (John 14:6). God's Word is truth, and Jesus is the fullest expression of God's Word. The Apostle John expresses the deep and wonderful truth that Jesus is God in the flesh, the incarnate Word of God. *In the beginning was the Word, and the Word was with God, and the Word was God* (John 1:1).

Jesus is the truth, the only way to a relationship with God the Father (John 14:6). When we trust Christ and receive the gift of salvation by grace through faith, we become people of truth. When Pontius Pilate asks that forlorn question about truth, it is in response to Jesus' statement, *"...I have come into this world to bear witness to the truth. Everyone who is of the truth hears My voice* (John 18:37). A person of truth is one who knows Christ and lives according to the truth of Scripture.

Remember, God's perfect love is always at the heart of His truth. As you read and ponder this chapter, keep in mind the following principles.

Truth matters because God is the only source of truth. We cannot place our hope in changing standards, earthly philosophies, vacillating opinions, or human reasoning. All of these things are shifting sand with no stability. God's Word, the Bible, is true and unchanging, and Jesus is God's Word in person. The two cannot be separated. If we know and love Jesus, we will know and love His Word.

Truth matters because truth is transformational. Jesus changes lives. He doesn't simply make people better; He changes us. The Apostle Paul writes...*it is no longer I who live, but Christ who lives in me* (Galatians 2:20). Scripture also says, *Therefore if any man is in Christ, he is a new creature; the old things passed away; behold new things have come* (2 Corinthians 5:17). When we trust Christ, He makes us a new creation. Everything about us is new—even the way we think and live.

When we know God through Christ, His Spirit begins to work on the inside of us. He is not interested in behavior modification or superficial adjustments to our lifestyle. He requires transformed thinking because what we believe and think always determines how we behave. God uses the Bible to transform our minds (Romans 12:2). It is the primary tool the Holy Spirit uses to accomplish an inward change, which is then expressed outwardly through the way we live.

Truth matters because truth overcomes darkness. Throughout Scripture, darkness and light are contrasted. Christ is the Light that cannot be extinguished by darkness (John 1:5). Likewise, God's Word is our guiding light as we seek to live in truth (Psalm 119:105). When we are transformed by the light of Christ and the light of His Word, we become lights in a dark world. Oh, how this dark world needs light. People everywhere are living in spiritual darkness. The Light of Truth is their only hope. We have that hope, and the Lord is asking us to be torchbearers of truth. Truth exposes and expels darkness *so let your light shine before men that they may see your good works and glorify your Father who is in heaven* (Matthew 5:16

Desperate for Truth

People are desperate for truth—whether they know it or not. Today's constant ebb and flow of thought and reason are evidence that the search for truth remains unfulfilled for many people. While the human soul has never been satisfied with

125

anything less than God's truth, mankind has sought a substitute for truth from the very beginning.

Adam and Eve had everything they needed, a perfect world and an intimate relationship with God. Yet they chose to believe the Serpent rather than believe God. They rejected God's truth and God Himself because they thought they needed more. John Piper writes, "Adam and Eve did not eat because they got hungry, but because their eyes had grown dim to God.... Eating (the fruit) was not the essence of evil because before they ate, they had already lost their taste for God."

As people of truth, how can we avoid losing our taste for God? How can we keep our eyes from growing dim toward God? How can we guard ourselves from the subtle yet destructive lies that permeate society? How can we wisely distinguish between accepted norms and God's holy standards?

Jesus understood that His followers, then and now, would live in a world filled with lies and confusion—so He prayed, *"Make them holy in Your truth; teach them Your word, which is truth"* (John 17:17 NLT). Likewise the Apostle Paul writes, *"Let the word of Christ richly dwell within you..."* (Colossians 3:16). The word *dwell* means to settle down and live. God's Word must live in us, finding a permanent and welcomed home in us, instructing us, and setting us apart as a holy people.

An alarming story is presented in 2 Kings 22-23. It jars me every time I read it. The astonishing story starts with an eight-year-old boy who becomes king. His name is Josiah, and Scripture says he did right in the eyes of the Lord (2 Kings 22:1-2). The account of Josiah is a warning to us, God's people of truth, to be on guard. Like the people in Josiah's kingdom, the lies surrounding us can become embedded within us if we minimize or disregard God's Word, if our eyes grow dim to God.

Josiah is a descendant of King David. His father and grandfather ruled as kings as did their fathers. In fact, David's lineage has secured the throne for over 300 years when young Josiah is anointed king of Judah. When Josiah becomes king, the nation of Israel has long since been divided, and the northern kingdom has already been conquered and destroyed by the Assyrians. Judah is the southern portion or southern kingdom, the only surviving area of the once great Davidic kingdom. Judah's capital city is Jerusalem, the Holy City where God has chosen to place His name. It is also where the Temple has been built—the only place of true worship.

God promised His servant David that David's descendants would always sit on the throne in Jerusalem (2 Samuel 7), but God's criteria for blessing would be based on their worship of God alone and their adherence to God's standards written in God's Law. Sadly, when Solomon succeeds his father David to the throne, he succumbs to idol worship, trying to please his many pagan wives. Idolatry gains a firm grasp on a nation who has toyed with it for generations. Consequently, centuries later, young Josiah inherits a kingdom saturated with profane idolatry and perverse living. When Josiah becomes king, the majority of God's people are no longer people of truth.

As king, Josiah doesn't have any godly examples to emulate. Josiah's father Amon ruled as king of Judah for only two years. The Bible says Amon was evil, following the wicked practices of his father before him. The wickedness of Amon was a carryover from Josiah's grandfather Manasseh, the most wicked king to ever sit on David's throne.

Manasseh seduced the people to serve and worship false gods—gods from the pagan Canaanite tribes that God had overthrown—gods that required child sacrifices and perverse sexual rituals as acts of worship. Manasseh erected idols inside God's holy temple. He practiced witchcraft, astrology, and divination. He welcomed male prostitutes into the Temple to assist with pagan worship. Furthermore, Scripture tells us that King Manasseh filled Jerusalem with innocent blood, slaughtering his own people and offering human sacrifices to false gods (2 Kings 21:1-18).

Manasseh led God's people to a new low. Their sins surpassed the godless nations surrounding them. Manasseh ruled for fifty-one years, and even though it seems he had a change of heart toward the end of his life, the damage was done (2 Chronicles 33). Sin had become so deeply embedded into the hearts of the people they abandoned truth and they ignored God.

Even though Josiah inherits a sin-filled mess, somehow his young heart leans toward truth. After ruling for eight years, sixteen-year-old Josiah begins to seek God. In spite of the corruption around him, Josiah yearns to know truth (2 Chronicles 34:3). Ten years later, when he is twenty-six years old, truth comes into focus.

In that day, every king of Judah had the responsibility of maintaining the temple built by Solomon. Josiah fulfills his responsibility and sets into motion the mundane task of renovating the sacred structure. The project, however, turns out to be anything but mundane. Shaphan the scribe and Hilkiah the high priest of God are overseeing the project when Hilkiah makes a shocking discovery.

Then Hilkiah the high priest said to Shaphan the scribe, "I have found the book of the law in the house of the Lord."
(2 Kings 22:8)

Think about this statement for a moment. Hilkiah, the high priest of God, has the holy responsibility of spiritually leading the nation. Yet somehow over the years, probably decades, God's Word has been lost—recklessly misplaced, stuffed into a storeroom or closet, buried under pagan relics right there in God's holy temple. More alarming than losing God's Law is the fact that no one even missed it. Hilkiah never missed it, so obviously he never taught from it or implemented it. The generation ruled by Josiah had never heard the Law of God and certainly never followed it.

Upon discovering the Book of the Law, Hilkiah gives it to Shaphan the scribe, and Shaphan reads it—maybe for the first time in his life. Obviously rattled, Shaphan goes to Josiah.

Moreover, Shaphan the scribe told the king saying, "Hilkiah the priest has given me a book." And Shaphan read it in the presence of the king. (2 Kings 22:10)

A book? Just a regular old book? Surely Shaphan's haste in taking it to Josiah indicates he has some idea that the book is God's written Word, the Pentateuch, which is the first five books of the Old Testament. As Shaphan reads, Josiah hears for the first time passages like these:

So watch yourselves carefully...lest you act corruptly and make any graven image for yourselves in the form of any figure, the likeness of male or female...And beware lest you lift up your eyes to the heaven and see the sun and the moon and the stars, all the hosts of heaven, and be drawn away to worship them.... (Deuteronomy 4:15-19)

*When you become the father of children, and children's
children and have remained long in the land, and act corruptly,
and make an idol in the form of anything, and do that which
is evil in the sight of the Lord your God so as to provoke Him
to anger, I will call heaven and earth to witness against you
today that you shall surely perish quickly from the land...
you shall not live long in it, but shall be utterly destroyed.*
(Deuteronomy 3:25-26)

*When you enter the land which the Lord God gives you, you
shall not learn to imitate the detestable things of those nations.
There shall not be found among you anyone who makes his son
or daughter pass through the fire, one who uses divination, one
who practices witchcraft, or one who interprets omens, or a
sorcerer, or one who casts a spell, or a medium, or a spiritist,
or one who calls up the dead. For whoever does these things is
detestable to the Lord...you must be blameless before the Lord
your God.* (Deuteronomy 18:9-13)

Additionally, Josiah hears for the first time the law of
God given to Moses on Mount Sinai. He hears the Ten
Commandments. He listens to the blessings of obedience
and the consequences of disobedience. He listens to God's
instructions about the importance of the Passover, the feasts,
and the festivals that serve as reminders of all that God has
done for His people. Through the reading of God's Word,
Josiah finally hears what his searching heart has longed for—
he hears truth. When he hears all that God has said, Josiah tears
his clothes in grief and fear, realizing how far God's people
have fallen, how far they have wandered from truth, how dim
their eyes have grown toward God (2 Kings 22:11).

Josiah quickly puts together a team of five trusted leaders and tells them to inquire of the Lord. The five leaders find a woman named Huldah, a reliable prophetess of God. She speaks hard words of truth to the listening men. Huldah tells the envoy that judgment is coming. God's wrath cannot be turned away from the people of Judah because they have forsaken the Lord and worshipped other gods. God says through Huldah, *"My wrath burns against this place, and it shall not be quenched"* (2 Kings 22:17b).

Huldah's message from the Lord to Josiah has two parts. First, Josiah the man is a sinner like everyone else; therefore, he must hear about the judgment of God that is coming soon. Second, Josiah the king will be spared from seeing God's judgment because his heart is tender, and he has humbled himself before the Lord (2 Kings 22:15-20).

When Huldah's message reaches Josiah, he acts quickly. He calls together the people of Judah and Jerusalem. He speaks to the crowd from the house of the Lord, and he reads the Book of the Covenant that was found in the temple. After he reads, Josiah leads by example, making a fresh covenant with God.

And the king stood by the pillar and made a covenant before the LORD, to walk after the LORD, and to keep His commandments, and His testimonies, and His statutes with all his heart and all his soul, to carry out the words of this covenant that were written in this book. And all the people entered into the covenant. (2 Kings 23:3)

With great resolve, Josiah immediately begins the arduous task of removing evil practices from the house of God and from the land itself. It is shocking to read how far the people have

131

strayed from truth and how great the task of stripping Judah of lies, superstition, perversion, and idol worship.

He orders the priests to remove from the temple all the vessels consecrated to Baal and Asherah. Baal is a false god of the Canaanites. Seven hundred years earlier when the Israelites entered the land, God strictly warned them not to imitate the followers of Baal. Now, vigorous worship of Baal is taking place under the same roof as lethargic worship of God. Likewise, Asherah is a false goddess, the female counterpart to Baal. The worship of Asherah involves perverse sexual acts. Her image is simply a stick, known as an Asherah pole. Josiah commands that any vessel used in the worship of these false gods be burned and the ashes carried away.

Josiah removes the vessels dedicated for worship of the sun, moon, and stars. He does away with the idolatrous priests who lead in the worship of Baal and Asherah and also those who practice astrology. He destroys the Asherah pole where unspeakable sexual acts are performed as acts of worship. Furthermore, Josiah tears down the tents set up to house male prostitutes—perverse men living in God's house, assisting worshippers with sexual exploits that have no boundaries. He removes the women who are making the tents for the male prostitutes. Josiah destroys an entire economic system of idol worship that has been allowed to prosper within the house of God.

King Josiah also kills the false priests who inhabit all the cities and villages of Judah. He tears down the altars to Baal and Asherah that are scattered over the countryside. The outdoor altars are called high places, and they provide convenient locations for false and perverse worship.

Josiah removes horses and chariots from the temple that have been dedicated to the sun god. He tears down perverse altars from the roof of the temple and from the inner courts of the temple. Then Josiah marches to Topheth, a place of burning in the Valley of Hinnom, and he tears down the most heinous altar and idol imaginable.

In the Valley of Hinnom, an idol of Molech, the detestable god of the Ammonites, had been erected. According to Jewish history, the idol was formed like a huge cylinder made of bronze with hollow bronze arms extended as if to cradle something. A fire was built inside the hollow cylinder causing the entire structure to glow with searing heat. A worshipper of Molech could bring an offering to the idol—the more valuable the offering, the closer the worshipper could get to the idol. If the offering was a child, the father of the child could metaphorically kiss the idol by laying his child onto the blistering hot arms of Molech.

The word Topheth comes from an Arabic word which means roaster. The word can also mean drum. Both definitions describe this hideous place of worship in the Valley of Hinnom. Jewish tradition states that the priests of Molech would wildly beat drums and dance with ecstatic cries so as to drown out the screams of a burning child. Some called Molech the laughing god because as the sacrificed child lay on the glowing hot arms of the idol, the child's skin would pull away from his or her tiny face, exposing the teeth, making it look as if the dying child was laughing.

I can barely breathe after writing these two paragraphs. It is difficult to fathom that these are God's people, the people God chose to be a holy nation, priests unto God, and a light to the nations. These are the people God set His love upon and this is the city of Jerusalem where God chose to put His temple and His Holy name. These are the people He rescued and fought for and led, a people He blessed with a lush and prosperous land. He provided for them and nurtured them like little lambs... and this is what they chose? This heinous worship is what they found more satisfying and trustworthy than God?

Josiah isn't finished. He breaks apart the altars that Solomon built on the Mount of Olives—altars to idols like Molech who accept child sacrifices. He puts to death mediums and witches and those who practice the occult. He burns household idols that litter the homes of God's people. Josiah also goes into the conquered and desolate land of the Northern Kingdom of Israel. He tears down and burns any remaining altars and high places. He slaughters the false priests who linger in the conquered territory.

Josiah not only removes perverse idols and evil altars from the land but also reinstates the Passover. The Passover has not been celebrated in over seventy years. Two generations have no knowledge of the holy feast. They have not been taught or reminded of God's great deliverance from Egypt.

While Josiah wholeheartedly sets out to purge the land from evil and bring the people back to God, reforms come too late for Judah. While God would always love His people and keep His covenant with them, He would not relent from judging their sinfulness.

And before him there was no other king like him who turned to the LORD with all his heart and with all his soul and with all his might, according to all the law of Moses; nor did any like him arise after him.
However, the LORD did not turn from the fierceness of His great wrath with which His anger burned against Judah, because of all the provocations with which Manasseh had provoked Him. And the LORD said, "I will remove Judah

from my sight also, as I have removed Israel. And I will cast off Jerusalem, this city which I have chosen, the the temple of which I said, 'My name shall be there.'"(2 Kings 23:25-27)

Josiah dies at the age of thirty-nine. Twenty-three years later, the Southern Kingdom of Judah is decimated by King Nebuchadnezzar of Babylon. The Jews who survive Nebuchadnezzar's ruthless military campaigns are carried away to Babylon, exiles and slaves for seventy years. God's people incur terrible consequences for their neglect of truth.

Truly, I have read and told and taught this story of Josiah for years, and it always horrifies and humbles me. It is not a far-fetched story from yesteryear. It is being lived out right in front of us in every culture and country, people living by their own truth. More alarming, however, is that the church—God's people, saved by grace, led and loved by the Redeemer—is quickly moving in the same direction as society.

Certainly, as people of truth, we may not exclude Christ altogether; however, our eyes can easily grow dim toward God, and our taste for truth can quickly wane. As Christians, we may not literally bow to idols, but what do we seek before we seek God's truth? What do we turn to, expecting it to give us what only God can give us? What have we allowed to coexist with Christ in our ideology, thoughts, opinions, or actions? Our idols may seem more sophisticated and intellectual than those of ancient times…but idols, whether ancient or modern, are always a substitute for truth. When we seek peace and satisfaction in anything other than Christ and His Word, lies begin to look like truth, God appears outdated, and souls once warmed by His grace grow cold to His Word.

I'm not trying to be dramatic. I am, however, trying to shake us out of indifference and neglect. If we say we love

Jesus, we must be able to say we love His Word. We must know and believe that what God says is true, allowing it to transform us from the inside out. Certainly, I am not writing to sway us toward ridged dogma void of love. Neither am I espousing legalistic adherence to rules and religion. God's Word is given to us with love; therefore, obedience to Christ and His Word brings freedom, not slavery.

Remember. The Christian life is not an esoteric experience. It is a relationship with God through Jesus Christ. God's people are a chosen people, set apart for His glory and His purpose. We are saved by grace, forgiven and redeemed, equipped by the Holy Spirit, and entrusted with the joy of making disciples. However, we will never live fully in our blessings apart from knowing God's truth and living it with an undivided heart.

Know Truth

Mrs. Iris Edwards graced our congregation in east Tennessee. Mrs. Edwards was a humble, senior adult woman of modest means. She loved the Lord and her family, and she served both faithfully. Mrs. E, as she was lovingly known, radiated with the love of Christ. While she had a quiet way about her, Mrs. Edwards attracted people, especially the growing throng of college students who were attending our church.

At Mrs. E's invitation, my late husband Dana would often swing by her house in the early morning for breakfast. Mrs. E loved her young pastor, and breakfast always included her encouragement and prayer. In one of their early morning meetings, Dana talked with Mrs. E about the students attending our church. As he was leaving her house, he asked if she would be willing to disciple a small group of female students.

Standing on her front porch, Mrs. Edwards cocked her head to one side, clearly not understanding Dana's request. "Dana, what do you mean by *disciple*?" He tried to explain, "You know. Teach them how to pray, how to spend time with the Lord, how to love God." Mrs. E was still perplexed, "Dana, how can you teach someone to fall in love?"

Her question has resonated in my mind for decades. Indeed, how do we fall in love with Jesus? And how do we teach others to fall in love with Him? The answer is not a program or curriculum. Without trying to oversimplify, falling in love with Jesus happens as we get to know Him. We better know and love Christ as we learn to know and love His Word.

Psalm 119 is a great place to start getting acquainted with His Word. While it is the longest chapter in the Bible, it is divided into twenty-two sections with eight verses in each section. The psalm is an acrostic, each section sequentially following the letters of the Hebrew alphabet. Throughout the psalm, the writer uses eight different words to describe Scripture. For you and me, however, the most notable aspect of Psalm 119 is that every verse speaks about the importance of God's Word in the life of a believer.

Whether you are a new believer, a long-time believer, or perhaps an unbeliever, reading Psalm 119, section by section over twenty-two days, is beneficial in understanding the depth and value of God's Word. I've listed some of my favorite verses from Psalm 119. You will want to mark and memorize your favorites as you read this treasured psalm on your own.

- *How blessed are those who observe His testimonies, who seek Him with all their heart.* (Psalm 119:2)
- *How can a young man keep his way pure? By guarding it according to Your word.* (Psalm 119:9 ESV)

- *I have treasured Your word in my heart, that I may not sin against You.* (Psalm 119:11)
- *Open my eyes that I may behold wonderful things from Your Law.* (Psalm 119:18)
- *My soul weeps because of grief; strengthen me according to Your word.* (Psalm 119:28)
- *Turn my eyes away from looking at what is worthless, and revive me in Your ways.* (Psalm 119:37)
- *And I will walk at liberty for I seek Your precepts.* (Psalm 119:45).
- *Teach me good discernment and knowledge for I believe in Your commandments.* (Psalm 119:66)
- *It is good for me that I was afflicted, so that I may learn Your statutes* (Psalm 119:71).
- *If Your Law had not been my delight, then I would have perished in my misery.* (Psalm 119:92)
- *Your word is a lamp to my feet and a light to my path.* (Psalm 119:105)
- *Establish my footsteps in Your word, and do not let any wrongdoing have power over me.* (Psalm 119:133)
- *Those who love Your Law have great peace, and nothing causes them to stumble.* (Psalm 119:165)

Mrs. Edward's question about falling in love may sound like a question based entirely on emotion. But knowing Mrs. E, her faith was not built on emotions. It was built on truth. Like any meaningful relationship, loving Christ and His Word takes time and intentionality. So, let's be practical about knowing Jesus more intimately by knowing and applying His Word.

Spend Time in God's Word. Jesus instructed His disciples to abide in Him and allow His words to abide or dwell in them

(John 15:1-11). Certainly, the practice of abiding cannot be boiled down to a small block of time or a devotional reading. Abiding is all consuming—thoroughly permeating us and completely transforming us. Abiding is intimate, but it must also be intentional. Remembering that our life in Christ is a relationship with Him helps us understand and apply principles of abiding.

If we are going to learn to abide in Christ and allow His truth to have a permanent home in our hearts and in our minds, we must make time for Him. While at first it may sound rigid, intentionally setting aside time for Bible reading and prayer is important. Abiding in Christ and knowing truth takes effort. Every relationship does—just ask the couple who has been married for fifty years. Remember Ray and Georgia Merritt from Chapter Two? Those love birds spent decades cultivating their relationship. Nothing of depth, especially relationships, happens haphazardly.

Again, I want this section to be very practical. The Holy Spirit will breathe life into our practical steps of obedience when we take the time to seek Christ and seek truth. I want to share with you some things that have worked well for me over the years. My methods of intentionally abiding may be different from yours, but perhaps this section of the chapter will give you a place to start if you have not already.

To begin, set aside a time, a place, your Bible, a notebook or journal, a pen, and a plan or guide for Scripture reading. Keep everything together in the place designated for spending intentional time with the Lord. This is just organizationally smart—not legalistic. As my place of meeting and reading, I have designated a chair in my living room with a small table beside it. Everything I need is right there. The room is quiet.

No television or computer is in sight, and my phone is put away or silenced. Distractions are avoided as much as possible. I don't even play background music while I am reading Scripture and praying. During this intimate time with the Lord, the goal is to be completely tuned in to hear from Him.

Before reading the Bible, write in your journal the date and the reference for the passage of Scripture you will be reading. Make a list of the things that are weighing on your mind, primarily the people and circumstances you want to pray about that day. Ask the Lord to clearly speak to you through His Word. With your mind moving in the right direction, pick up your Bible and read.

Each day, I use a reading plan or guide to help me read the Bible in an organized manner. The passages of Scripture I read are not long, usually no more than a chapter and most days significantly less. Without a reading plan, I would be all over the place, uncertain of what to read, never wanting to read the hard stuff, and never venturing into unknown territory of passages I don't understand. Typically, when there is no organized plan of reading Scripture, it is easy to gravitate to the same familiar passages over and over. Without a plan, it is also easy to get discouraged and quit altogether. A plan builds consistency and expands our knowledge of Scripture.

There are many reliable Scripture reading plans easily accessible in printed form or through some means of technology. When looking for a plan or a guide to assist you in Scripture reading, look for one that requires you to open your Bible and read the verses. Some devotional books print the designated verses trying to streamline the process. However, having passages of Scripture printed for us can be limiting, discouraging us from handling God's Word by ourselves. Likewise, no sentimental story or a writer's personal illustration will substitute for actually reading Scripture.

The Bible I use for daily Bible reading is *my* Bible. I mark it, write notes in the margins, and underline verses. I have to admit—I'm old school. I like a physical copy of the Bible. I know smart phones and tablets are convenient and useful for Bible reading, but to me the pages of Scripture are beautifully sacred. It's my opinion to be sure, but one I hope you will consider.

Another thing to consider is the time of day for Bible reading and prayer. I like the early mornings, but that hasn't always been the case. After my first child was born, my daily schedule was turned upside down. It seemed I never had a moment for myself, and if I did, the stack of laundry or the sink full of dishes called louder than any quiet moments with the Lord. I felt defeated and neglectful, so I prayed. I sincerely asked the Lord for a solution, asking where in my day could I find time to spend with Him. Almost immediately, I sensed the Lord working.

In the chaos of my day, when it seemed I had no control over my schedule, I would notice a fifteen-or-twenty-minute reprieve—a time when the baby was sleeping or contently occupied. I learned I could spend those available minutes with the Lord, or I could tackle a household task. However, if I chose to do anything other than spending that small window of time with the Lord, I wouldn't have another opportunity to do so during the day. Truly, there was no guilt heaped onto this solution, just a choice I could make with the time I believe the Lord provided for me each day.

Some days that window of time was in the mornings, but not often. Most of the time, I noticed a few minutes in the early afternoon would suddenly clear for me. At other times, the middle of the night became a sacred time of quiet, drawing me to pray and read the Bible. Thankfully, that chaotic season of newborns passed, although I have discovered each season of life has its own time-management challenges. Some people say early morning is the only appropriate time for a devotional time, but in my opinion, any time is a good time to read God's Word and pray. As we prioritize time with the Lord, the time becomes a cherished blessing rather than a learned discipline.

In our daily time with the Lord, reading the same passage of Scripture several times helps plant it into our minds. The primary objective in reading Scripture is to understand what God is revealing about Himself. Knowing God is our purpose in all of life. We only know God as He reveals Himself to us, primarily through His Word—so read with a sensitive and alert mind.

As Scripture becomes more familiar, read with a curious mind as well. Knowing the author, the original audience, and the historical circumstances gives greater understanding and enjoyment as we read. A study Bible or a good reading guide will help answer some of these questions. As we engage in meaningful Scripture reading, training our minds to ask questions and seek answers, we discover that truth has depth and purpose far beyond a feel-good quote for the day.

After reading the passage of Scripture several times, write down your own insights. I'm not suggesting pages and pages of notes, rather a simple summation of the facts with an emphasis on the character, words, or works of God. For a few minutes, meditate on what Scripture is revealing about God. As you think about the character of God in the context of the day's reading, allow God's Word to work in your heart and mind.

The Holy Spirit will use the Word of God to convict of sin, encourage, teach, train, and give wisdom (2 Timothy 3:16-17). Be still and allow God's Word to soak into your soul. Be quick to yield to whatever God is saying through His Word. Write a few sentences in your journal as a reminder of the work God is doing in you through His Word. Finally, using the verses you have read, the insight you have gained, and the list of concerns you have listed—pray.

Prayer is a beautiful overflow of spending time in Scripture. Sadly, many have come to believe that prayer requires an expansive vocabulary, specific theological training, or a special prayer language. Sometimes prayer is viewed as an opportunity to present a wish list to God. None of these things are true. Prayer is the verbalization of a surrendered life. It is simply talking with God.

Applying Scripture to our prayers is helpful in verbalizing our thoughts and concerns to God. It also gives us confidence that we are praying God's will. Likewise, it keeps our prayers fresh when we pray often, perhaps years, for the same concerns. Praying truth goes hand in hand with reading truth.

Several years ago, I was given a simple acrostic for the word PRAY. **P...praise, R...repent, A...ask, Y...yield**. While I rarely advocate a formula for any spiritual discipline, I will readily pass along any tool that helps believers as they grow in the Lord. Following this simply acrostic helps organize scattered thoughts and also helps incorporate Scripture into our prayers. Likewise, praying out loud helps us remain focused. As you pray, try using the acrostic to apply the passage of Scripture you have read to the list of concerns you have written in your notebook.

Praying God's truth is life giving. It keeps us from simply

reading and then quickly forgetting what we have read, never applying it to real-life situations and needs. Praying God's Word gives direction to our prayers and guards us from selfish praying. Over the years I have prayed for the same family members repeatedly, sometimes feeling like my prayers have grown stale. However, praying for those family members using God's Word breathes new life into my praying.

Remember, abiding in Christ and allowing His Word to abide in us is a relationship that is cultivated, not an exercise in legalism. There is no formula that fits every person and circumstance. Spending time in daily Bible reading and prayer is a beginning point to expand and build upon. As you grow in love and knowledge of Christ, consider additional ways to incorporate truth into your life.

Memorize Scripture. Memorization builds a storehouse of Scripture the Holy Spirit can use at any time, bringing to our minds what we have hidden in our hearts (Psalm 119:5,9,11,92,105, Psalm 1).

Study the Bible. In addition to daily reading, learn to study, asking curious questions and digging deeply to understand the Bible as a whole. Invest time in a group Bible study where study skills can be strengthened and applied to personal times of study (2 Timothy 2:15).

Listen to Truth. In a world filled with technology, there are countless opportunities to fill our minds with truth. Sermons, podcasts, seminars, and classes are readily available. Also, songs and hymns filled with truth can encourage and teach us. As you seek God's truth from a variety of sources, always keep in mind the Bible is the straightedge by which everything is measured. Anything we put into our minds must be evaluated based on Scripture, not opinions or persuasive words (Psalm 119:98-99, 130, Philippians 4:8, Colossians 2:2-4).

There are no shortcuts to abiding in Christ and allowing His Word to abide in us. Yes, at first it takes time and practice and effort—every relationship does. The results, however, are life-changing: maturing us, satisfying our need for truth, and always drawing us closer to Christ, who is the lover of our souls.

Live Truth

While there are practical steps to implement as we learn to abide in Christ and His Word, we must be clear in our understanding of truth. Knowing and loving truth is not an intellectual pursuit that has no bearing on the way we live. Abiding in Christ and allowing His Word to abide in us is a life to be lived empowered by the Holy Spirit.

The Apostle Paul often describes the Christian life as our walk—our daily living as a new creation in Christ. Sadly, for many Christians there is a discrepancy between the truth we profess to believe and the way we live. In his book *Do You Believe?* Paul David Tripp writes,

I could give example after example of a dichotomy that exists in so many of us (and still exists in some places in my own life) between what we say we believe and the way we live. And I am persuaded that the gap between the doctrine we say we believe and the way we actually live is a workroom for the enemy. What I am going to say next may surprise you, but I think it needs to be said and considered. The enemy of your soul will gladly give you your formal theology, if in your real daily life he can control the thoughts and motives of your heart and, in so doing, control the way you act, react, and respond. (17)

Twice the Apostle Paul admonishes his readers to *walk in a manner worthy of the call* (Ephesians 4:1, Colossians 1:10). The Greek word *worthy* means in perfect balance. Paul is saying we are to live in perfect balance with our call to salvation. We are to live as Christ has commanded us to live, outward testimonies of a changed life. Living in perfect balance with our wonderful salvation will always be a contrast to the world's way of thinking and living.

Ephesians 4-5 gives us five "walk statements" that describe the way we are to live as Christ-followers.

*...**walk** in a manner worthy of the call with which you have been called, with all humility and gentleness, with patience, showing forbearance to one another in love, being diligent to preserve the unity of the Spirit in the bond of peace.* (Ephesians 4:1-3)

*...**walk** no longer just as the Gentiles (unsaved) walk....* (Ephesians 4:17)

*...**walk** in love, just as Christ has also loved you....* (Ephesians 5:2)

*...**walk** as children of light....*(Ephesian 5:8)

*...**walk,** not as unwise men, but as wise.* (Ephesians 5:15)

These words can be overwhelming if we take them seriously. In fact, on our own and in our own strength, this worthy walk is impossible. However, the Lord equips us to live as He has commanded us to live. He graciously gives the

Holy Spirit, permanently dwelling within us to empower us and to equip us for living (Ephesians 1:13-14, Ephesians 3:16, Matthew 14:16-20, Matthew 16:5-15, Ezekiel 36:26-27).

The Holy Spirit is often misunderstood, but Scripture teaches He is the third person of the Trinity, the Spirit of the Lord Jesus Christ given in full to every believer at the moment of salvation. He is a permanent resident within the believer, readily available to empower us for right living. We may temporarily ignore Him or grieve Him, but we cannot extract Him from our lives. He is the seal of our salvation, signifying a permanent transaction—the eternal exchange of our unrighteousness for the righteousness of Christ (Ephesians 1:13-14, 2 Corinthians 5:21).

The Holy Spirit lives within every person who knows and loves Christ, but how do we as believers in Christ utilize the wonderful gift of the Holy Spirit? How does the Holy Spirit enable us to live as new creations? The answer to these questions has a practical yet profound answer: we participate with the Holy Spirit. We trust and obey.

In his book *The Transforming Power of the Gospel*, Jerry Bridges uses the phrase *dependent responsibility* to describe our relationship and response to the Holy Spirit (105). We are totally dependent on the Holy Spirit to strengthen us to live the Christian life. We are also completely dependent on Him to produce any good fruit in our lives. However, we are responsible to cooperate with the Spirit, humbly obeying Him as He leads us and instructs us. Paul describes dependent responsibility perfectly in Philippians 2:12-13.

Therefore, my beloved, as you have always obeyed, so now, not only as in my presence but much more in my absence, work out

*your own salvation with fear and trembling, for it is God who
works in you, both to will and to work for His good pleasure.*
(ESV)

A crusty East Tennessee man described these verses as
"the holy want to." God's Spirit gives us the desire to please
God as well as the ability to please God. Please remember, our
obedience does not earn any part of our salvation. Trusting God
enough to obey Him is our response to His gift of salvation.
As we daily choose to lay aside the old way of living and put
on the new way of living, the Holy Spirit empowers us to do it
(Ephesians 4:22-24, Colossians 3:2).

Living the Christian life is inextricably connected to the
truth of Scripture. The Holy Spirit uses God's Word to teach
us what pleases God. He uses God's Word to instill wisdom
and understanding in us, to strengthen us, and to bear good
fruit in our lives (Colossians 1:9-12, John 5:1-11). In Scripture,
spiritual fruit is anything that pleases God. Only the Holy
Spirit can produce fruit, and He produces good fruit as we love
Christ, love His Word, and live to serve Him.

Trusting and serving Christ, empowered by the Holy Spirit
and guided by truth, is where we experience lasting joy and
abundant life (John 10:10). Unfortunately, many Christians
are searching for a grand experience, an exciting ministry,
a public sign, or a miracle to signify the depth or reality
of their Christian life. The Christian life, however, is best
demonstrated in a quiet, consistent walk of faith—trusting God
enough to obey Him. God is not asking us to do exciting things
for Him. He is asking us to live in a way that pleases Him—to
live as people of truth (Colossians 1:10-12).

In Conclusion

In King Josiah's day, the people of Judah were searching
for something additional, something more spectacular than God
and His Truth. Over the years, their obedience and love for God
became dull, overshadowed by fleshly pleasure. Superstition
was substituted for truth. The sun and stars, brass idols, and
wooden poles were worshipped instead of Almighty God. All
of this happened because God's people moved away from truth
instead of toward it.

Precious reader, moving away from truth doesn't happen
overnight. Once-vibrant Christians can inch away from truth,
growing cold gradually. We can incrementally substitute
current trends and popular philosophies for life-giving truth.
Sadly, if we minimize God's Word, we can quickly find
ourselves lingering in the darkness, and as our eyes slowly
adjust to the darkness, they will simultaneously grow dim to
God.

God is calling His people back to truth. He is inviting
us to drink deeply from His Word, to embrace all of it
wholeheartedly as the loving and authoritative revelation of
God. There is no substitute for truth and there is no new truth—
there never will be. Certainly, our understanding of truth will
grow and expand as we know Christ more intimately, allowing
His Word to abide in us, transforming our thinking and our
living. Remarkably, however, we can spend a lifetime learning
and loving truth and never unearth all of its treasures.

Knowing truth and living truth have far-reaching impact,
not only on us but also on the people we love and the world
around us. We are commissioned to share the truth we
have experienced (Matthew 28:19-20). We are called to be

torchbearers, taking the light of truth into a dark world through our love-saturated words and deeds. Why? Because the world is desperate for truth. Just look around. People are searching for truth, and they are filling the void with things that will never satisfy their souls. Only truth fills the void. Only the truth of Christ satisfies the soul.

The person who loves truth *will be like a tree firmly planted by steams of water, which yields its fruit in its season, and its leaf does not wither, and in whatever he does, he prospers* (Psalm 1:3).

Truth makes a difference in those who love it. It always has. It always will.

Discussion Questions
Desperate for Truth

1. Read Psalm 1. Discuss the benefits of knowing and loving God's Word. Discuss the contrast between those who love God's Word and those who do not?

2. From a young age, King Josiah yearned to know truth. How does he learn truth? What does he do with the truth he learns? What are we responsible for doing with the truth God reveals to us in Scripture?

3. An idol is anything we turn to, expecting it to give us what only God can give us. What are some things we often turn to expecting to find lasting joy, peace, contentment, or security?

4. In a society that often rejects God's truth, how can believers in Christ discern truth from lies?

5. Discuss how we can practically read and apply God's Word. If someone is new to reading the Bible, why is an organized plan important? Would you share any methods of reading Scripture that have been helpful to you?

6. A believer in Christ is responsible for living in God's truth, and yet no one can live the Christian life in their own strength. Discuss the role of the Holy Spirit as we daily seek to live in truth. (John 14:26, John 16:13-14, Ephesians 3:16)

Endnotes

For over twenty-five years I have used a daily Bible reading guide from a ministry called *Scripture Union*. *Scripture Union* produces two different guides. *Encounter with God* is a guide for people who are already familiar with Scripture. *Discovery* is a guide for those who are new to daily Bible reading. Both guides are available online. They are also available in print for a reasonable yearly subscription.

There are many good Scripture reading guides available online or in print. You may already have a plan that works for you. If not, I recommend the material produced by *Scripture Union*. For years I have shared *Scripture Union's* contact information with my students and readers.

info@scriptureunion.org
www.scriptureunion.org

Scripture Union USA
P.O. Box 215
Valley Forge, PA 19481
1-800-621-LAMP

5

DESPERATE
For Hope

Anticipating a coming disaster can shake us. At this very moment I am writing from a hotel room having evacuated with my husband from our home. Our coastal community is anticipating a massive hurricane that could alter the lives of thousands of people.

After my husband and I prepared our house, prayed, shed a few tears, and heeded the warning to get out, we left our hearts behind. Certainly, the leaving rattles our nerves, but it also brings renewed clarity about temporal things. The gravity of the approaching storm makes unimportant things glaringly unimportant. The desperate circumstances also turn our eyes to God alone—the only source of hope as we wait for the coming storm.

Habakkuk is God's prophet, and he is also waiting for a storm. Like many of us, in the waiting, he is desperate for hope.

The prophet Habakkuk lived around the same time as the prophets Jeremiah and Ezekiel. He experienced the reforms implemented by Josiah, and he also saw those reforms quickly fade after Josiah's death. Habakkuk penned his short but profound book during the reign of Jehoiakim, Josiah's younger son. Habakkuk is classified as a minor Old Testament prophet, not because he is less important, but because his writing is brief.

The entire three-chapter book of Habakkuk is a conversation between the prophet and God. Initially, Habakkuk brings a complaint to God and God replies. However, God is not giving Habakkuk an explanation. Instead, He is giving the troubled prophet a new perspective. Like so many other passages of Scripture that deal with the subject of suffering and hope, the focus is not about *why*—it is about *who.*

The book of Habakkuk is a gem of a book. It contains several familiar passages and is often quoted by New Testament writers. For me, the message of Habakkuk is personal. It was a favorite study for my late husband, and it has been a source of encouragement for me in overwhelming and seemingly hopeless circumstances. I have run to this book often, always having my perspective adjusted and my faith strengthened. Like the other chapters of *Living on the Edge of Desperate,* this chapter is not a verse-by-verse study of Habakkuk. While I typically like outlines, we will work our way through the three chapters of Habakkuk using a series of questions. Regardless of the format, my greatest desire is for God's Word to guide us toward the hope that is ours in Jesus Christ.

What is hope?

The prophet Habakkuk begins his book by asking age-old questions. *Why do the wicked prosper? Why is evil prevailing? Why is God silent about it all?* It seems Habakkuk is discouraged as Josiah's reforms fade, exposing the true nature of a people who claim to know God. In the midst of bad circumstances—that will get decisively worse, Habakkuk needs hope. In fact, he is desperate for hope.

Hope is one of those words we use often in Christian circles, but rarely define. While the word *hope* appears over one hundred times in the Bible, modern usage of the word has departed from its Biblical meaning. Before we define Biblical hope, let's explore what hope is not.

- Hope is not wishful thinking or a wishful sentiment. (I hope you are well. I hope it is a good day. I hope it doesn't rain.)

- Hope is not positive thinking. It is not coming up with a plan, crossing our fingers, or even praying fervently in an effort to will our positive thoughts into being.

- Hope is not our perception of how things should be or the way we want them to be.

- Hope is not based on emotions. If it is based on emotions, we have hope when we feel hopeful, and we are hopeless when the feeling of hope is absent.

Biblical hope is based on truth—the unfailing, unchanging Word of God. The New Testament Greek word for hope is *elpis.* The same word is used often in secular Greek and means *a desire for something good.* The Biblical meaning of *elpis* has a fuller and richer meaning.

Biblical hope is the desire for something good and the confident expectation that we will receive it based on the Word of God and the character of God. In other words, everything God has said in His Word, we can be confident that God will do it.

As Christians, our hope is bound to Christ. Our relationship with God through Jesus Christ is our assurance that God will accomplish everything He has promised. Every spiritual blessing is ours in Christ (Ephesians 1:3). Every promise God has given to us is a resounding *YES* because of Christ (2 Corinthians 1:20). Because we have Jesus Christ, we have everything we need for life and godliness (2 Peter 1:3). Indeed, Christ is our hope (1 Timothy 1:1).

The hope we have as believers in Christ anchors our souls (Hebrews 6:19). Our soul is the sum total of all that we are as human beings: the integration of our mind, emotions, will, desires, personality. We don't have a soul—we are a soul. Hope keeps our soul anchored when life shifts and changes.

When storms prevail, sickness persists, death intrudes, relationships disappoint, crisis overwhelms, or fear looms— hope remains sure and steadfast because Christ Himself is our hope. Certainly hope does not exempt us from difficulties. It does, however, grip us in the middle of the difficulties. A wonderful truth to remember during times of trouble is that we do not have to muster up enough strength and fortitude to hold onto our hope. Hope holds onto us, and nothing can snatch us out of His hand (John 10:28).

Implementing our hope into everyday living is always linked to faith. Hope is a part of faith. Hebrews 11:1 states,

"Faith is the assurance of things hoped for, the evidence of things not seen." Hope is forward facing, expectation with confidence. Faith is a daily exercise in trusting and obeying Christ. Let me give you a few examples of how faith and hope work together.

We are told in 1 John 1:9, *"If we confess our sin, He is faithful and righteous to forgive us our sins and to cleanse us from all unrighteousness."* What a wonderful promise! This is our hope, our confident expectation that if we confess our sins, He will forgive us and cleanse us. Now we must apply faith to that wonderful promise. We must trust the Lord enough to obey Him. We must actually confess our sins to Him and trust that He forgives us. By faith, we allow Him to clean out the sinful areas of our life. When we participate in God's promises by faith, we are living in our hope.

Another example of hope and faith working together is Philippians 1: 6. This verse tells us *"...He who began a good work in you will perfect it (mature it) until the day of Christ Jesus (His return)."* Again, what a wonderful promise, a great hope. God started the work of salvation in us, and God will continue to work in us every day, until that work is mature and complete. Now, we must apply faith to this wonderful hope-filled promise. In faith, we cooperate with the Holy Spirit each day, surrendered to Christ, growing in our love and knowledge of His Word. In faith, we must be willing to trust and obey the Lord as He matures us. We live in our hope as we exercise faith.

Habakkuk looks around at the bleak circumstances and his troubled soul needs hope—hope that God has not forgotten His people, hope that God has a plan, hope that there is a future to look forward to. Certainly, God will adjust Habakkuk's perspective, but Habakkuk must respond in faith to God's message. He must trust God's heart even though God's reply is not what Habakkuk is expecting. For Habakkuk, and for you and me, hope and faith always work together.

Where do we go when we feel hopeless?

Habakkuk writes during the reign of King Jehoiakim, the second son of Josiah. Jehoiakim's reign follows the death of his older brother Jehoahaz, who only reigned for three months before being killed by the Pharaoh Neco, king of Egypt. Jehoiakim is selected by Pharaoh Neco to rule Judah as a vassal state, one that answers to Egypt. Egypt imposes heavy taxes on Judah, and Jehoiakim ruthlessly extracts the taxes from the people of Judah.

While Habakkuk's countrymen are experiencing heavy taxation from the king, they are also experiencing unmerciful extortion from wealthy Hebrew landowners who threaten to take land from the poor. Additionally, the courts and ruling officials of Judah are accepting bribes from the wealthy so that when a poor person is cheated out of his land or money, there is no recourse in the legal system. Injustice is being carried out against the people of Judah by their own people. Egypt may have a heavy hand on Judah and king Jehoiakim, but brother against brother is where the greatest cruelty is being played out.

When Habakkuk writes his book, it is a chaotic and oppressive time for the people of Judah. It is under these discouraging circumstances that Habakkuk cries out to God. Habakkuk's cry takes the form of a complaint, a questioning of God's character and credibility and a doubting of God's care and concern for His people. Habakkuk may not be railing at

God, but in his lack of understanding, the prophet is accusing God of turning the other way while evil prevails.

How long, o Lord, will I call for help and You will not hear?
I cry out to you, "Violence!" yet You do not save. Why do You
make me see iniquity and cause me to look on wickedness?
Yes, destruction and violence are before me; strife exists and
contention arises. Therefore the law is ignored and justice is
never upheld. For the wicked surround the righteous, therefore
justice comes out perverted. (Habakkuk 1:1-4)

In previous chapters, we discussed Job's questions and David's laments, but Habakkuk's prayer is different. His cry contains an underlying disappointment with God. The prophet seems to think God is not credible or true to His own covenant. In the Old Testament, the unique role of a prophet is to be a spokesperson for God. Habakkuk is not only questioning God, but also questioning his own role as a prophet. After all, how can a prophet speak on behalf of an uncaring God?

Because of the violence and wickedness surrounding him, Habakkuk feels hopeless. If God won't intervene, then who will? Certainly, the people of Judah will not listen to Habakkuk if the God he represents is idly standing by, doing nothing to correct injustice. While Habakkuk can be commended for turning to the Lord with his complaint instead of turning away from the Lord, it is obvious that the prophet is having a crisis of faith. While his world is quaking, Habakkuk needs an anchor. He needs hope.

I can't be too hard on Habakkuk. I have had my own crisis of faith, feeling hopeless and concluding that God's silence shows a lack of care. After the shock of my late husband's death subsided, the reality of the loss set in. Everything in my life was turned upside down, and I felt like fear was suffocating me. Keep in mind I was a Bible teacher and a minister's wife at the time of my husband's death. I knew the Scriptures and could readily grasp that God was sovereign and mighty. However, in my grief, I could not grasp that He loved me and cared about the details of my life. For a brief season, I felt hopeless.

Perhaps all of us have experienced the empty feeling of hopelessness. When life isn't turning out the way we imagined, hope may seem to be in short supply. But it isn't. Hope is always available for the believer in Christ.

Our hope is tied to the faithfulness of the Lord, not our circumstances or our feelings. There is a huge difference in *feeling* hopeless and *being* hopeless. Feelings come and go, but hope remains. It anchors our souls while the storms rage. As Christians, we cannot lose our hope because Jesus Christ is our hope. He will never leave us or forsake us. He is the rock we run to, lean on, and hide in. Certainly, our feelings can betray us, but our Saviour never will.

While we cannot lose our hope, we can choose not to live in it. We refuse to live in hope when we take our eyes off of Jesus and follow our feelings instead of the truth of Scripture. The New Testament book of Hebrews says we can choose to embrace what is ours in Christ and be encouraged (Hebrews 6:18). On the other hand, we can choose to live by our own reasoning and be like waves tossed about by the wind (James 1:6).

Living in our hope requires faith, trusting God enough to obey Him. It may also require a change of perspective, an adjusting of our attitude and outlook even while difficult circumstances remain.

Certainly, the Lord is merciful when we struggle with feelings of hopelessness. With great love, He reaches into our pit and turns our face toward His precious son Jesus, our Hope. God will eventually turn Habakkuk's face toward hope, even as circumstances grow worse for Judah. God will give the complaining prophet a fresh perspective of who God is, even if Habakkuk initially has a limited understanding of the *why*. God will do the same for us. Be encouraged. Christ is our unshakable hope, even while the edge of desperate is our temporary camping ground.

My soul, wait in silence for God only, for my hope is from Him. He only is my rock and my salvation, my stronghold; I shall not be shaken.
On God, my salvation and my glory rest; The rock of my strength, my refuge is in God.
Trust in Him at all times, O people; pour out your heart before Him.
God is a refuge for us. (Psalm 62:5-8)

How can we live in hope when we don't understand what God is doing?

God hears Habakkuk's complaint, and unlike the story of Job, God answers Habakkuk immediately. However, God's reply will not satisfy Habakkuk's questions. In fact, God's response in Habakkuk 1:5-11 will raise more questions. The first few phrases probably capture Habakkuk's attention immediately.

Look among the nations! Observe! Be astonished! Wonder!
Because I am doing something in your days—you would not
believe if you were told. (Habakkuk 1:5)

If we only read verse 5, it seems that God is taking their
conversation in a positive direction. As God begins speaking,
perhaps Habakkuk feels relieved, sensing God is following
Habakkuk's gameplan after all. God will clean up the mess
in Judah, punishing the wealthy landowners and the corrupt
politicians. The poor will be vindicated. The country will be on
the right path. Judah will be great again.

It seems that hope—as Habakkuk defines it—is on the
horizon. God's plan, however, is nothing like Habakkuk's.

God's plans are rarely, if ever, like ours. He has a different
perspective. He is infinitely wise. He charts the course of
eternity. He knows what we need is different from what we
want, and in great love, He gives us what we need. We often
wrestle with God's plans because we prefer our limited, self-
constructed, human plans. Even if our plans are not sinful or
decisively selfish, they lack God's perfect eternal perspective.

Habakkuk will be shocked, even terrified, by God's plans.
God's course of action, however, will not be deterred. His
purpose and plans will not be thwarted (Proverbs 19:21, Isaiah
46:10). While God carries out His eternal plan, He will do a
good work in Habakkuk. God will move Habakkuk from fear
to faith, from feeling helpless to being hopeful.

Instead of resolving the immediate problems in Judah, God
tells Habakkuk that He will judge the entire nation of Judah for
their ongoing sinfulness. God will raise up the Babylonians,
a fierce world power, and He will use them as His rod of
discipline and justice against Judah.

God describes the Chaldeans, or Babylonians, as impetuous, dreaded, and feared. He describes their horses as swifter than eagles and keener than wolves. He paints a verbal picture of warriors swooping down on their prey. He warns the prophet that the merciless Babylonian army will violently march into Judah. They will seize homes, take captives, mock kings, laugh at fortresses, and leave a wake of destruction like Judah has never seen. Finally, after Babylon has served God's purpose, He will hold the Babylonians accountable for their pride. God will eventually judge those whose strength is their god (Habakkuk 1:7-11).

Secular history as well as Scripture gives us more detail about the Babylonian invasion of Judah and Jerusalem (2 Kings 24-25, 2 Chronicles 36:5-21, Jeremiah 52). At the time of Habakkuk's writing, Babylon is ruled by King Nebuchadnezzar. Nebuchadnezzar ruled Babylon, which is modern day Iraq, for over fifty years. He never lost a military battle. His conquest of Judah and his decimation of Jerusalem was carried out over a twenty-year period through three distinct military campaigns. Each military campaign intensified until the city of Jerusalem and God's temple were completely destroyed in 586 B.C. The majority of the people of Judah were either killed or carried away to Babylon as captives. God's people remained in captivity for seventy years. Many scholars believe Habakkuk survived the invasion and was taken into Babylon, never to return to his homeland.

Hearing about the imminent invasion could have evoked anger in Habakkuk. Instead, it softens him. He knows the heart of God, but in this moment, he cannot understand the ways of God. In Habakkuk's mind there seems to be a contradiction between God's holiness and God's actions. The perceived contradiction creates a tension within Habakkuk. With sincerity, Habakkuk ponders aloud to God (Habakkuk 1:12-17).

Habakkuk has a clear understanding of God's holiness, knowing God cannot and will not do anything evil. He also understands that God is using the Babylonians to discipline the people of Judah. This judgment, however, seems so severe, so final. In dispensing judgment, will God overlook the cruelty of the Babylonians? Will He allow the invading nation to get away with unchecked wickedness? Surely, God still loves His people. Surely, God will not wipe out His people completely.

A thorough study of the Babylonian invasion might lead us to agree with Habakkuk. The discipline God brings on Judah is intense. Certainly, God is wise and loving, but He is also holy. Because He is holy, He hates sin—especially in the lives of His people. While it seems the Babylonian invasion is a severe method of judgment, we must remember the sins of Judah are severe. It takes tough measures for God to get through to His hardhearted people. His goal, however, is not vengeance. His goal is to restore His people to a right relationship with God.

The Babylonian invasion and the subsequent seventy-year captivity is God's judgment on Judah for their wickedness and their neglect of God. Re-read the story of Josiah. Examine the horrifying deeds the nation of Judah normalized and applauded. Add to their moral perversion the corruption of the wealthy and the oppression of the poor. God has been patient and merciful towards His people for centuries. Habakkuk's initial complaint to God couldn't be further from truth. God has never overlooked evil. He has grieved over every sinful act His people have ever committed. Now, He is preparing to judge sin and discipline the nation.

Listen carefully. The believer in Christ may experience

the discipline of God (Hebrews 12:6-11). Discipline is correction—setting us on the right path. While discipline seems unpleasant, the purpose of God's discipline is to train and mature us, not punish us. Christians may experience God's discipline, but a Christian *will never experience God's judgment for sin.*

Jesus endured God's judgment against sin once and for all when He died on the cross (Hebrews 7:25-27, 9:12). His precious blood paid the price for our sin (1 Peter 1:18-19). Because of Jesus' death and resurrection, we are justified—our sin debt is paid in full (Romans 3:23-24). The good news continues because in exchange for our sinfulness, God's gives us the righteousness of Christ, changing us forever...making us a new creation and children of God (1 Corinthians 5:17, 21).

God is the same God in the Old and the New Testament. The price of sin has always been death. God established this truth from the beginning. Out of love and care for His people in the Old Testament, He gave the sacrificial system as a way of covering the sins of His people. It was a system that involved the death of a lamb as a substitute for man's sin. It was also a system that foreshadowed the death of His Son, Jesus Christ, the prefect Lamb and the perfect substitute for our sin. For believers, the cross is not only a humbling demonstration of God's love but also a powerful display of God's judgment of sin.

To God, there is nothing dismissive about sin. God has been patient with Judah. The coming judgment at the hands of the Babylonians is not a quick-tempered or rash decision. It is God's holiness and great love mingled with His sorrow and faithfulness. Redemption is the ultimate goal, and agape love is at the heart of it. Redeeming sinful people has always been and will always be the heart of God.

After the coming judgment, Habakkuk will not live another seventy years to see the completion of God's redemptive actions. He will not live to see the Babylonians overthrown by the Medes and Persians. He will not live to see Ezra and Nehemiah lead the captives back to their homeland. He will never see the walls around Jerusalem restored or God's temple rebuilt. It is possible Habakkuk has heard or read the message of hope from his contemporary Jeremiah, but God does not give Habakkuk every detail about the future. Habakkuk will have to trust the heart of God, even when he does not understand the ways of God.

For thus says the Lord, "When seventy years have been completed for Babylon, I will visit you and fulfill My good word to you, to bring you back to this place. For I know the plans I have for you," declares the Lord, "plans for welfare and not for calamity, to give you a future and a hope. Then you will call upon Me and come and pray to Me, and I will listen to you. And you will seek Me and find Me, when you search for Me with all your heart. And I will be found by you...and I will bring you back to the place from where I sent you in exile." (Jeremiah 29:10-14)

If we want to live in hope, we must trust the heart of God even when we don't understand His ways. Like Habakkuk, there is often a tension within us when what we know about God seems to collide with what God is doing—or not doing. Even in the tension, hope remains. The character of God is steadfast. We can trust His heart, His wisdom, and His unfailing love. We can choose to respond to the Lord with faith, exemplified by a humble and obedient life. When we cannot see the end result of what God is doing now, we still have hope. God never changes. He does not lie. He will accomplish everything He has promised.

What does God desire from us, even when we are shaken by circumstances?

There is nothing Habakkuk can do to change the coming tsunami of events. Without a complete understanding of the *why*, Habakkuk begins focusing on the *who*. He stations himself and waits for God's second reply (Habakkuk 2:1). Habakkuk has no plan to offer God and no further questions. He simply stands still. While his insides are trembling, Habakkuk listens for God's voice.

When circumstances are out of our control, our natural tendency is to find a solution to the problem and implement it quickly. We like action and results. We want the conflict to end swiftly and the conflict resolution to be in our favor. Simply being still seems counterproductive. However, when all of life is shaking—God's voice is heard when we are still. If the edge of desperate clamors for action, be still. In your stillness, be reminded that God remains sovereignly in control. A.W. Tozer is credited with saying, "Although it looks like things are out of control, behind the scenes there is a God who has not relinquished His authority."

God is our refuge and strength, a very present help in trouble, therefore we will not fear, though the earth should change, and though the mountains slip into the sea: though its waters roar and foam, and the mountains quake at its great swelling... **Be still** *(cease striving) and know that I am God....*(Psalm 46: 1-3,10)

While Habakkuk is still and silent, God speaks for the second time. He gives the prophet instructions to follow. God also gives assurance that the Babylonians will be held accountable for the atrocities they will inflict on Judah. It must have been difficult for the prophet to comprehend that the very nation God empowers to judge Judah's sin will also be judged by God (Habakkuk 2:2-20). The age-old tension between the sovereignty of God and the free will of man is once again presented. God's sovereignty and man's freedom to choose are presented throughout Scripture. They are parallel truths that never intersect, and God never explains. To God, there is no tension between the two.

With fresh perspective, Habakkuk surrenders his questions and concerns to Sovereign God. Even though he knows the days ahead will get worse before they get better, Habakkuk chooses to trust God and do whatever is asked of him.

Then the Lord answered me and said, "Record the vision and inscribe it on tablets, that the one who reads it may run. For the vision is yet for the appointed time; it hastens toward the goal, and it will not fail. Though it tarries wait for it; for it will certainly come, it will not delay.
Behold, as for the proud one, his soul is not right within him: But the righteous will live by his faith...." (Habakkuk 2:2-4)

Habakkuk is given four instructions:

1. **Habakkuk must write down the vision.** Habakkuk is told to write down the message and vision exactly as God has given it to him. He cannot soften up or minimize the severity of God's coming judgment. The

170

LIVING ON THE EDGE OF DESPERATE

message must go out to the people of Judah with clarity and truth.

2. **Habakkuk must wait.** There is no escaping the coming judgment, and there is no amount of preparation that can ward off the destruction. Habakkuk must be still and wait, even if the vision tarries. Although two years pass before the first wave of Babylonians come, God is true to His word. The vision is fulfilled at the appointed time—God's time. Habakkuk cannot rush it or hold it back. He must trust God completely with the details and the timing.

3. **Habakkuk must live by faith.** Faith requires trusting God enough to obey Him, even though Habakkuk knows death and destruction are just ahead. He also understands that life will never be the same for God's people. Even though the future looks grim, Habakkuk trusts God's plan and God's heart.

4. **Habakkuk must trust God with a future he will not live to see.** God promises to deal with the ruthless Babylonians. Their wickedness will not go unchecked. God pronounces five judgments or "woes" on Babylon (Habakkuk 2:6,9,12,15,19). Habakkuk will not live to see any of these judgments come to fruition. He simply must place his hope in the faithfulness and sovereignty of Almighty God.

God's instructions to Habakkuk are not easy, nevertheless, Habakkuk obeys. He does what God asks him to do. He writes, he waits, and he trusts—facing uncertain days with renewed hope and faith in The Almighty. Habakkuk gives up any thought of going back to life as usual. Instead, he chooses to keep his eyes on God no matter what may come. Habakkuk chooses to trust and obey.

Trust and obey. This is what God asks of us as well—even when we are shaken by circumstances. Keep in mind that God never called us to a life of ease. He calls us to follow Him no matter where He leads and no matter what circumstances we encounter. While life may never be our idealized version of normal, we can continue to live in hope as we trust and obey the Savior.

During a recent season of uncertainty, Psalm 23 became very dear to me, especially verse four. *Even though I walk through the valley of the shadow of death, I fear no evil, for You are with me...* (Psalm 23:4).

Recently, my husband Allen faced a serious health crisis. We have known for years that he suffers from a liver condition for which there is no cure. However, because of his ongoing condition, cancer developed on his liver. We were told that without a liver transplant, his prognosis was grim. The news sent us spinning with a thousand questions and emotions. While the diagnosis was unsettling to both of us, I became fearful, envisioning life as a widow—again.

For weeks, we drove back and forth to the hospital, an hour's drive each way. At every appointment Allen endured a myriad of tests, bloodwork, poking and prodding, ups and downs, good news and bad. It seemed the entire process was not only physically grueling for him but also an emotional roller coaster, relentlessly jerking both of us in unexpected directions.

At the same time Allen was enduring medical tests, I was teaching a Bible study for the women of our city. The study focused on God's peace and included many of the Psalms. It has always struck me as both humorous and terrifying that when the Lord leads me to teach on a subject, He also requires me to live it out—in living color for everyone to see. Each week I stood to teach about God's peace while my insides were battling fear.

One particularly discouraging week at the hospital was also the week of Bible study that included Psalm 23. *The Lord is my shepherd, I have all that I need* (Psalm 23:1). The problem was, I had a lot of needs! I needed peace and hope and faith. I needed the Good Shepherd to put me in a quiet, green pasture—and fast. Allen and I had already been through several dark valleys, and I certainly did not want this one for either of us.

In the stillness of study and prayer that always precedes teaching, the Lord, the Good Shepherd, began to speak to my fearful heart.

Psalm 23:1-3 assures me of the Shepherd's guidance and provision; therefore, He will never abandon me in the valley of deep darkness. In fact, He chose this valley for Allen and me, and only He knows the way through it.

Even though the valley of deep darkness is frightening, He will not allow me to take a shortcut, nor will He provide an easy exit. He leads me through the valley and He leads at His own pace. The psalmist writes, *Even though I walk through the valley.* I am reminded that if I am walking then He is also walking because He is the one leading me. While I would rather run ahead or run back or run away, He stays the course— walking, taking His time, doing a much-needed work in me. As I walk, He is teaching me to trust His pace and His purpose.

The Good Shepherd, not the ease of the journey, is where I find hope and peace. In the dark valley of uncertainty, I can abandon my fears because He knows the way through the wilderness. All I have to do is follow.

Allen and I had many discussions about our future while driving back and forth to the hospital. There was no sugar-coating the seriousness of his condition. We both had fears that Allen might not survive. We also knew God could heal him. The choice we made was to trust and obey, to follow the Shepherd…no matter where He leads.

Six months after the initial diagnosis, doctors told Allen that his untreated cancer had miraculously diminished and could no longer be classified as cancer. At this time, they concluded Allen no longer needed a transplant. On the other hand, the serious condition that caused the cancer remained unchanged; therefore, the possibility of cancer returning remained as well.

Where did the mixture of good and hard news leave us? Right where we had always been—in the Shepherd's care. Today, Allen and I are still rejoicing in God's mercy and the good report from doctors. We are also living in the reality that only God holds tomorrow. The dark valley experiences remind us that hope and peace, even joy, are not tied to pleasant circumstances. They are blessings from God, given freely as we entrust ourselves to Him.

For Habakkuk, the storm clouds of judgment are gathering, but Habakkuk waits with hope. Faith is the key. This is God's desire for every believer, even if our world is shaking. Trust and obey.

May the God of hope fill you with all joy and peace as you trust in Him, so that you may overflow with hope by the power of the Holy Spirit. (Romans15:13 NIV)

Trust in the Lord with all your heart, and do lean on your own understanding. In all your ways acknowledge Him, and He will make your path straight. (Proverbs 3:5-6)

Lord, will you help me live in hope, even when life is hard?

The final chapter of Habakkuk's book resonates with hope. Chapter Three is a prayer written in the form of a highly emotional psalm. It may have been written at a later time than the first two chapters of his book. It was written for worship gatherings, perhaps to sing in anticipation of what would come. The final verses of the song are some of my favorite verses in all of Scripture.

Habakkuk is trembling as he writes. He trembles with awe and reverence for Jehovah. He also trembles because he knows devastation is approaching (Habakkuk 3:2,16).

Let me be clear. Fear is not the opposite of faith. Pride is the opposite of faith. Pride is self-reliance, believing we know more than God. It is the original sin that has infected all of mankind since the beginning (Genesis 3). Humility, on the other hand, is declaring our total dependence on Christ. Only humble hearts exercise faith in the Lord.

Habakkuk has been emptied of the pride he exhibited at the beginning of the book. Now, even though he is trembling, humility responds with hope and faith. In spite of his initial complaint to God, Habakkuk becomes a marvelous example to follow. As we read Habakkuk 3, our faith is strengthened, not because the days ahead will be easy but because God is faithful...no matter what happens.

Habakkuk's opening words of the psalm are a statement

175

of faith as well as a request for mercy. He speaks directly to Yahweh, the LORD, the covenant-keeping God. God chose Israel long ago to be His people. They were set apart to live holy lives, dramatically different from the people around them. God's people would be a light to the nations, and from His people God's Messiah would come. God's plan of redemption for mankind would come through His people. Habakkuk is asking God to revive His work in His people, even while they experience exile. Habakkuk is also asking for mercy while God carries out judgment and discipline (Habakkuk 3:2, Deuteronomy 7: 6-9).

Following his request for mercy, the once doubting prophet beautifully extols the holiness, majesty, and power of God. Indeed, creation displays His splendor. The whole earth sings His praises. Plagues and pestilence obey His command. His power is unrivaled. Nations tremble before Him. God alone is the Eternal One (Habakkuk 3:3-7).

Habakkuk also reviews what God has done for His people in the past. God has delivered them from their enemies. He has parted seas and rivers for their safety and benefit. He has come against those who try to take advantage of His people. Habakkuk's imagery reminds them of God's ongoing deliverance. The reminder will instill hope for the long years ahead.

You marched across the land in anger and trampled the nations in Your fury. You went out to rescue Your chosen people, to save Your anointed ones. You crushed the heads of the wicked and stripped their bones from head to toe. (Habakkuk 3:12-13 NLT)

Dear reader, when you are living on the edge of desperate and tomorrow seems hopeless—remember! Remember who God is. Review the truth of Scripture. Read the mighty stories of God's power and redemption. Rejoice in the beauty and majesty of His creation. Rehearse His promises. Recall His great love, His salvation, His forgiveness, and His grace. Recount events from your past when you have experienced His faithfulness and His goodness. As you remember all these things, allow Him to renew your hope. God is still God. He will keep every promise. He will never leave you or forsake you.

Three times the word *selah* is inserted into the emotional song (Habakkuk 3:3,9,13). *Selah* means to rest. In an ancient worship song, it was a musical pause. Today, if your heart is trembling—pause. Meditate on who God is and what He has done. Hope is renewed as we set our minds on the Eternal One who has always been sovereignly in control.

The final stanza of Habakkuk's psalm is powerful. It overflows with strong emotion and shining hope. Human emotions and steadfast hope do not necessarily contradict each other. Habakkuk is facing the future with both. His words will encourage us to do the same.

I heard and my inward parts trembled; At the sound my lips quivered. Decay enters my bones, and in my place I tremble. Because I must wait quietly for the day of distress, for the people to arise who will invade us. (Habakkuk 3:16)

Habakkuk is trembling, but he is not distraught. He is not seeking an escape from the coming day of distress. His quiet waiting does not imply passivity or despair. Even though emotions are strong, Habakkuk has confidence in

God. His perspective has changed. Instead of looking at the circumstances around him, Habakkuk's focus is the LORD.

Living in hope is not cavalier or unemotional. God never asks us to be nonchalant about the difficulties of life. He has created us with emotions, and He does not chide us when they come to the surface. We will rarely, if ever, face difficult days with little or no emotion. When Scripture admonishes us to *cease striving*, God is not telling us to ignore our emotions, pull ourselves together, and slap a smile on our face. Instead, He is reminding us to relinquish our need for control and trust Him (Psalm 46:10).

Quiet waiting requires knowing where to turn when the pressure is on. If we turn toward our inconsistent emotions, they can take over and drive us to despair. An often ignored fruit of the Spirit is self-control. Self-control is disciplined emotions—emotions yielded to the Holy Spirit's control (Galatians 5:22-23). God has not created us to be robots, void of feelings. Emotions are a blessing, a God-given outlet of expression. However, unbridled emotions can quickly lead us into trouble.

Like Habakkuk, quiet waiting turns us toward God. The prophet Isaiah writes more than one hundred years before Habakkuk, but he writes under similar circumstances as Habakkuk. *In returning and rest you shall be saved; in quietness and in trust shall be your strength* (Isaiah 30:15). Turning back to God or turning toward God demonstrates trust. As we submit our emotions to the control of the Holy Spirit, we allow ourselves to be anchored in hope. Interestingly, God's supernatural peace always accompanies hope (Romans 15:13, Philippians 4:6-7).

Truthfully, some days our hope will be mingled with tears. Sometimes we will turn toward the Lord with our hearts racing and adrenaline pumping. At times we will wrestle with fear. Certainly Habakkuk has a sense of foreboding, but he does not surrender to it. He is surrendered to Jehovah, who is his hope. Likewise, living in our hope requires surrender to Christ, trusting Him even when emotions rise to the surface.

I want to reiterate two things. First, I said earlier that fear is not the opposite of faith. Pride is the opposite of faith. Fear is a natural and common emotion that can come upon us suddenly in stressful circumstances. It can even serve as a warning, helping us avoid danger. Fear, by itself, is not sinful. However, succumbing to fear and allowing it to dictate the way we live is sinful. Scripture addresses the subject of fear often because it is not only a common emotion but also a powerful emotion. Over time, fear can easily become our default setting. However, standing firm in truth, allowing our souls to be anchored in hope, and choosing to trust Christ are spiritual weapons of destruction, tearing down any fortress fear tries to build (2 Corinthians 10:3-5).

Second, trusting God is not a one-time decision. We choose to trust moment by moment, day by day. In minor annoyances or cataclysmic tragedies, we cooperate with the Holy Spirit, entrusting ourselves to our sovereign, wise, and loving Heavenly Father. Also, trusting God is never passive. It is active, demonstrated through everyday obedience (Psalm 37:3-4).

The prophet Jeremiah lived in Jerusalem and preached during the same time as Habakkuk. Like Habakkuk, he knows God's judgment is coming through the Babylonians. He preaches hard truth to the people of Judah about judgment and repentance. He also preaches hope, reminding the people of God's love for them. The promises of God recorded by

Jeremiah reach far into the future—even beyond the seventy years of captivity. God's promises include a new covenant and a righteous Branch, the Messiah. The promises will unfold in God's time, but they will surely come to pass.

Habakkuk would have heard and read the words of Jeremiah. The final chapter of Habakkuk's book assures us that Habakkuk fully embraced the promises of God recorded by Jeremiah. By the time Habakkuk writes his psalm, his roots of faith are deep. He is no longer seeking a good outcome somewhere down the road. He is simply trusting God, with hope.

Then after seventy years are completed, I will punish the king of Babylon and that nation, the land of the Chaldeans, for their iniquity, declares the LORD, making the land an everlasting waste. (Jeremiah 25:12 ESV)

For behold, the days are coming, declares the LORD, when I will restore the fortunes of my people, Israel and Judah, says the LORD, and I will bring them back to the land that I gave to their fathers, and they will take possession of it. (Jeremiah 30:3 ESV)

"...you will be My people, and I will be your God." (Jeremiah 30:22)

"...and they shall return from the land of the enemy. And there is hope for your future," declares the LORD. (Jeremiah 31:16)

"...this is the covenant which I will make with the house of Israel after those days," declares the LORD, "I will put My

*law within them, and on their heart I will write it; and I will be
their God, and they will be my people. "* (Jeremiah 31:33)

*Behold a day is coming, declares the LORD, when I will fulfill
the promise made to the house of Israel and the house of
Judah. In those days and at that time I will cause a righteous
Branch to spring up for David, and He shall execute justice
and righteousness....And this is the name by which it (the
Branch) will be called: The LORD is our righteousness.*
(Jeremiah 33:14-16 ESV)

Our hope is not based on pleasant outcomes or happy
endings to the difficulties of life. Our hope is in Christ. We
experience the peace that accompanies hope as we surrender
to His purpose, His plan, His ways, and His timing. We are not
idly waiting for the valley to end or the crisis to be averted.
Instead, we are expectant, anticipating that God will do
whatever He wants to do...whenever He wants to do it. Even
if our insides are shaking and even if we do not see the fullness
of His promises until we arrive at Heaven's gates, we can live
today in hope—confidently trusting and obeying Him.

Read Habakkuk's beautiful closing words. Store them in
your heart for the days ahead.

*Though the fig tree should not blossom, and there be no fruit on
the vines,
Though the yield of the olive should fail, and the fields produce
no food,
Though the flock should be cut off from the fold, and there be
no cattle in the stalls,
Yet I will exult in the LORD,*

I will rejoice in the God of my salvation.
The Lord God is my strength, and He has made my feet like
hind's feet,
And makes me walk on my high places. (Habakkuk 3:17-19)

I love these verses. They ring with hope. Three times the prophet writes *though or even though. Even though* unimaginable destruction will come, Habakkuk will rejoice in the Lord. He will live with confident hope. Certainly, Babylon will strip Judah down to a wasteland, but Habakkuk turns his face toward the Redeemer who will not abandon His people.

Many times, I have wept while praying my own version of Habakkuk's words. *Even though* I experience great loss…the Lord is my strength. *Even though* the diagnosis is cancer…I will rejoice in Christ . *Even though* my children wander…. He is my salvation. *Even though… even though…even though.* Everything around us may seem bleak, …but our God is always with us and for us. He is working out His perfect plan in His perfect time, not only in our lives but also in all of eternity.

Examine thoughtfully the analogy Habakkuk uses of a sure-footed deer walking in treacherous places. Older English translations use the word *hind*, which is a poetic word for a female deer. Any deer hunter will tell you the female deer is more timid and cautious than the male. In Habakkuk's song, the typically cautious deer walks with confidence on high places because God created the deer for rough terrain and craggy mountains..

Living near the Appalachian Mountains for many years, I observed a few things about mountains and high elevations. Mountains are beautiful, but they are not necessarily safe.

182

Mountains have perilous cliffs and rocky pathways. There can be unforeseeable danger from rock slides or floods. In addition to the rough terrain, winds can be fierce and the weather can be inclement at high elevations.

In the Christian life, we commonly use the metaphor of mountains and valleys. Valleys are a description of dark and difficult circumstances in life, whereas mountain tops represent the exhilarating and joyful experiences. Habakkuk's poem presents a different perspective—high places are good places, but often they are hard places too. Remarkably, like the deer, the Lord has designed us to walk confidently in hard places. Hannah Hurnard writes in her book *Hind's Feet on High Places*, "He has designed us to walk on the rocky cliffs as if they are asphalt roads."

God never promises smooth journeys and easy outcomes. He certainly never promised Habakkuk these things, yet when we read the prophet's final phrases, we hear hope. It would be unreasonable to think fear never enters Habakkuk's heart again. I'm sure it does. The invasion of Judah and the destruction of Jerusalem would be brutal. Habakkuk is human, but his focus and his confidence is the LORD.

It is also unreasonable for Christians to label anything that is hard or painful as bad. We cannot confuse a good life with an easy life. Hard things can bring good results when we surrender all of it to the Lord. God is in every detail, working all things together for good—His definition of good—for those who love Him (Romans 8:28).

Many times God's greatest good will take us to hard but beautiful places. The poetic description of the timid deer skipping along the dangerous cliffs gives us hope. Certainly, our confidence is not in our own ability to navigate trials. Our confidence is in Jesus Christ—God with us and in us.

Like the hurricane I mentioned at the beginning of this chapter, the storms come. They bring destruction and loss. Judah's storm comes as well. But dear one, God is in the storms. He is our strength, allowing us to live confidently even in difficult circumstances. In Christ, the edge of desperate is a place of hope.

Behold I will do something new, now it will spring forth: will you be aware of it?
I will even make a roadway in the wilderness, rivers in the desert. (Isaiah 43:19)

Discussion Questions
Desperate for Hope

1. Describe the difference between the modern usage of the word hope and the Biblical definition?

2. Read Hebrews 11:1-2. Discuss how hope is linked to faith. If hope anchors our soul when life shifts, what role does faith play?

3. Read Habakkuk 1:1-4. The prophet Habakkuk is having a crisis of faith. What circumstances give him a feeling of hopelessness? When you look around at the world today, can you relate to his feelings?

4. God's plans are different from what Habakkuk expected. Give an example of a time when God's plans for you were different than your self-constructed human plans.

5. God gave a promise to His people in Jeremiah 29:10-14. How does this help Habakkuk trust the heart of God even when he doesn't understand what God was doing? Is there a passage of Scripture that has been meaningful to you when you have not understood the ways of God?

6. In difficult times, Psalm 46:1-3,10 challenges us to *Be still and know that I am God. Being still*, however, does not mean being passive or inactive. What instructions does God give Habakkuk while he waits (Habakkuk 2:2-4).? What does God ask of us in season of waiting?

7. Habakkuk's closing words in Habakkuk 3:17-19 encourage us. His beautiful analogy of the sure-footed deer gives us hope. Discuss these verses. What stands out to you as you read them? While we prefer happy endings and pleasant circumstances, what is God teaching you about His hope in difficult times? Are you experiencing His hope in your present circumstances?

6

DESPERATE
For Mercy
John 8:1-11

It's early morning when Jesus enters the Temple.
A crowd immediately gathers, eager to hear Him teach—
anticipating a message unlike the rigid dogma of the Pharisees.
They have come to hear news of a kingdom that offers rest for
their weary souls and relief from the burden of religion.

On this morning, however, the much-anticipated teaching
of Jesus is suddenly interrupted. A woman is cast before
Jesus, brought against her will by a brood of Pharisees. She
is disheveled and inappropriately dressed for the Temple. Her
hair is uncovered, and her eyes are downcast. The crowd leans
in to hear the accusation and watch the teacher's response.

The Pharisees, policing even the bedrooms of the

unsuspecting, caught her in the very act of adultery. A secret tryst is now a public spectacle. Even though her guilt is obvious, both the woman and the crowd know the religious leaders have no inclination for justice. The Pharisees are using her as a tool. She is simply carnage in their ongoing battle with Jesus. With trembling resolve, the woman listens for a verdict. Expecting to hear condemnation, this desperate woman cannot fathom an encounter with mercy.

God's mercy permeates every page of Scripture. Even when the word *mercy* is absent, His heart of mercy is present. God's ever-present mercy is never diminished or overshadowed by any other attribute of God. Even His justice, holiness, and righteousness are fully exercised while His mercy remains. Like a multifaceted diamond, every attribute or characteristic of God remains completely unobstructed by another. Each facet of His perfect character works in perfect union, demonstrating God's matchless glory. However, as we zero in on the depth and cost of God's infinite mercy, I pray we will see its brilliance and it will take our breath away.

Because the word *mercy* is a common word, especially in religious circles, it will serve us well to distinguish its Biblical definition from its common usage. Oxford Dictionary defines *mercy* as compassion or forgiveness shown to someone whom it is in one's power to punish. This is a good definition, but let's put it into a Biblical perspective: God's mercy is compassion in action. It is His tenderhearted approach to His people— His never-ending kindness toward us. God's mercy recognizes our need and is moved to meet our need. In the context of both salvation and sin, His mercy is not only compassion in action, but it is also withholding the judgment we deserve.

Also keep in mind the following:

1. God's mercy is not weakness. He never exercises His mercy from a position of weakness or as a last resort when all else has failed.
2. God's mercy is not simply a feeling. God is not feeling sorry for us when He extends mercy to us.
3. God's mercy does not ignore sin or the consequences of sin. His mercy works in tandem with forgiveness and redemption.
4. God's mercy is not cheap. It comes to us at a high cost.
5. God's mercy is not limited or exhaustible.

In Scripture, we find other words that are synonyms or descriptions of His mercy: *compassion, loving kindness, kindness, goodness,* and *good will* are just a few. Both the Old and New Testament speak often of God's mercy. It is a mistake for us to view God as wrathful in the Old Testament and merciful in the New Testament. His mercy is boundlessly present in both.

In the Old Testament, there are several Hebrew words for mercy. One is the Hebrew word *chesed.* It is found throughout the Old Testament but used extensively in the Psalms. It is often translated *lovingkindness,* but can also be translated *love, unfailing love, compassion, or faithful love.* I remember taking a class in seminary, studying the psalms. My professor said there is not an exact translation for the Hebrew word *chesed.* Because of the richness of this Hebrew word and the extreme depth of love and mercy implied, translators have struggled to convey its meaning. While we do not use the term *lovingkindness* in our everyday speech, I believe it captures the Hebrew meaning well. Officially, *chesed* is defined as an attitude of love which contains mercy.

Psalm 136 uses the Hebrew word *chesed* repeatedly. The psalm is an antiphonal song. In Biblical times, the worship leader would read a line of truth, history, or an act of God, and in response, the people would say, *"His mercy (chesed) endures forever."* To our modern ears, Psalm 136 may sound redundant, but in ancient worship the repetition grew in intensity each time the people responded to the worship leader. It was a celebratory experience, solidifying in their minds the goodness and faithfulness of God.

One of my favorite passages of Scripture is Lamentations 3:22-23. I have run to these verses many times in my life, remembering the Lord's mercy never fails. Dear reader, these verses are for you too. Run to them with confidence knowing His mercy never dries up or goes away. In our sin, our doubts, or our shortcomings, the Lord is faithful to love us and extend mercy to us. His mercy is unexplainable, but it is ours through Christ. What a treasure we have!

Because of the Lord's faithful love we do not perish, for His mercies never end. They are new every morning; great is Your faithfulness. (Lamentations 3:22-23 CSB)

Another Hebrew word for mercy is *racham*. This Hebrew word was used extensively, but not exclusively, in the writings of the prophets. *Racham* conveys the idea of love and compassion even in times of severe discipline. Over and over in the Old Testament, God would discipline His people. However, neither His discipline nor His judgment was void of mercy. Remember, one attribute of God is never diminished by another—they operate in perfect union.

An interesting distinction of the word *racham* is that it usually refers to a strong love within a natural bond, like a parent and child or a husband and wife. An example of *racham*, translated *lovingkindness and compassion*, is Isaiah 54:8.

"In an outburst of anger I hid My face from you for a moment; But with everlasting lovingkindness I will have compassion on you," says the Lord your Redeemer.

Finally, we must give special attention to a third Hebrew word *kipporeth*, translated *mercy seat*. This very special word is used twenty-seven times in the Old Testament and is always used to describe the golden cover or lid of the Ark of the Covenant. The sacred Ark was housed in the Holy of Holies, deep inside the tabernacle and later in the temple. The mercy seat is where God promised to meet His people. The high priest would enter the Holy of Holies once a year on the Day of Atonement (Yom Kippur) and sprinkle the blood of a sacrificed lamb on the mercy seat to atone for the sins of the people. Make no mistake, the blood of every animal in the world would not wipe away sin, but God in His great mercy chose to accept the sacrifice and cover their sins. Year after year (Exodus 25:21-22, Leviticus 16, Micah 6:6-8).

Listen carefully. Everything in the Old Testament points us to the New Testament. The mercy seat is a foreshadowing of Jesus Christ. He is our mercy seat. He is where we experience the mercy of God. His blood has been applied not to the golden cover of an ark, but to our very lives—forgiving our sins and covering us with His righteousness. We are made right with God because Jesus paid the price for our sin, spilling His precious blood at Calvary for us (Leviticus 17:11, Romans 6:23, 1 Peter 1:18-19, Romans 3:25, Hebrews 9:26-27, Hebrews 10: 4, 9-12, Hebrews 10:18-22).

It's clear God's mercy punctuates every page of Scripture. We see His mercy in the Psalms, the writings of the prophets, the temple ordinances, and in the lives of His people. The Old Testament is saturated with His mercy. But dear one, when we see Jesus in the New Testament, we see with even greater clarity the compassion of God. Jesus is God with skin on, and He is the pinnacle of God's lovingkindness toward us.

Throughout Scripture God's mercy is always intentional, purposeful, and redemptive. He does not extend mercy out of pity or weakness; He extends mercy to redeem us. His merciful kindness toward us is the catalyst for forgiveness. It draws us in. It clears the path for grace and right relationship with God the Father. We cannot underestimate or ignore the depth of God's mercy, made available to us through Jesus Christ.

Mercy Applied to Sin and Shame

The woman hurled at Jesus in John 8 is guilty of adultery. After all, they caught her in the very act. Some commentators believe she had been caught days or weeks earlier and now the Pharisees are simply revisiting the accusations against her. However, since John is careful to include the detail that it is early morning when Jesus enters the temple, it makes sense that she has been caught in the very act that morning or at some time during the night (John 8:2).

Regardless of when she was discovered, she is not in the temple of her own free will. Furthermore, she is Jewish and knows the potential consequences for adultery. It doesn't take much of an imagination to understand she is a woman in distress, filled with fear...and consumed with shame.

The Pharisees have an agenda. They want to prove that Jesus is a false teacher, and they will attempt to use the Mosaic Law and this woman to make their point (John 8:4-5). They have no compassion for the guilty woman, no regard for the authority of Jesus, and evidently a shortsighted interpretation of the Law. Obviously, it takes two people to commit physical adultery. The Pharisees are well-aware of Leviticus 20:10 and Deuteronomy 22:22, which state both the man and the woman are to be judged and, if found guilty, stoned. But on this morning, they have singled out the woman. The religious leaders are also aware that the occupying empire of Rome would never allow the chaos of a Jewish stoning. It seems Rome has no regard for the Mosaic Law. If Jesus disagrees with the Mosaic Law, He is a heretic. If He concurs with the Law, He is at odds with Rome. The trap is laid.

The scene is contentious and heated. Emotions are running high. This is not a private or secluded confrontation. The crowd, the woman, and the Pharisees are waiting for Jesus' response. The tension is thick, but instead of verbally responding, Jesus silently stoops to write in the dust.

We are not told what Jesus writes or even if He writes anything legible at all. It seems Jesus purposefully pauses, allowing the gravity of the situation to sink in. Jesus is giving the Pharisees an opportunity to realize the gravity of their accusation. Likewise, He is giving the woman time to ponder the gravity of her sin. The uncomfortable pause hangs heavy, perhaps defusing some of the emotional electricity. Still the Pharisees continue to press Him for an answer. All eyes are on Jesus. Finally, Jesus stops writing in the dirt. Addressing the

Pharisees, He stands and speaks:

He who is without sin among you, let him be the first to throw a stone at her. (John 8:7)

Jesus isn't looking for a sinless person to throw a stone at her. He is looking at a group of religious men and saying, *"He who is without **this** sin."* Adultery can be committed in the mind and heart of a person as well as with the physical body. Jesus knows they are all guilty to some degree of the very sin the woman is accused of. As the truth silently sets in, Jesus' second phrase hits its mark.

"Let him be the first to throw a stone at her." The incessant questioning by the Pharisees stops. Jesus has not only reminded them of their own sin, but He is using the Law of Moses to foil their plot. Deuteronomy 17:6-7 requires two or three witnesses to condemn a guilty person to death by stoning. Furthermore, the witnesses must be the first to throw a stone, starting with the oldest witness.

Jesus isn't challenging the Pharisees. He isn't puffed up with chest out, exerting His authority saying, "I dare you!" Jesus is simply letting truth do its job. He is allowing time for truth to penetrate their sinful hearts. Every person who hears Jesus' timely words understands their own guilt—especially the oldest and presumably wisest witness and especially the accused woman.

Again, Jesus stoops to write in the dirt. Again, the weighty pause has an effect. The Pharisees realize they have lost this battle. Surely, they already knew Rome would not overlook a Jewish stoning, but now they understand the Law of Moses doesn't condone their actions either. Quieted, the religious leaders slip away. The oldest ones, acutely aware of their inability to perfectly keep the entire Law, leave the scene first. The other religious leaders follow. The curious crowd backs away. Jesus is alone with the woman.

For the second time in the narrative, Jesus stops writing in the dust. He stands and speaks, but this time He speaks only to her. *"Woman, where are they? Did no one condemn you?"* (John 8:10)

Jesus nor the woman is denying her guilt, yet somehow no condemnation has occurred. To condemn means to pass judgment, but shockingly the voices accusing her have been silenced, and the stones meant to kill her have been abandoned. How can this be? What kind of teacher is this? Will He pronounce His own brand of judgment on her? Will there be retribution or perhaps penitence to pay? With a hundred questions swirling through her mind, she cautiously replies, *"No one, Lord"* (John 8:11a).

"Neither do I condemn you; go your way; from now on, sin no more." (John 8:11)

In my mind, I can hear her gasp. Mercy has spoken. Mercy has pardoned. Jesus passes no judgment on her, no condemnation. While He has the authority to condemn her, with compassion He forgives her instead.

Make no mistake. Jesus is not sweeping her sin under the rug. He is not downplaying her guilt. He is not excusing the offense. He is pardoning her, and that pardon will soon cost Jesus His life. He will die for that woman's sin of adultery and every other sin in her life. He will pay the price for her sin, taking her punishment on Himself. But His mercy doesn't stop with forgiveness. It paves the way for grace that redeems.

Jesus tells the woman to *"go your way; from now on, sin no more."* Notice the order of Jesus' words to her in John 8:11. First, He pardons. Then He tells her to sin no more. Religion will always reverse that order. Religion tells us to get our act together. Stop sinning. Make your life right…*and then* you will be good enough for a relationship with God; *then* you will be good enough to ask for His mercy. Friends, religion has it all wrong. Mercy earned is not mercy at all.

For the woman and for us, God's mercy and compassion usher into our lives the mighty work of grace. Grace that redeems, making us new and empowering us to live in a new way. Mercy isn't powerless pity. God's mercy is life-giving and redemptive because His mercy is inextricably linked to His grace.

We are all guilty. Every person is born a sinner. We do not become sinners when we commit our first sinful act. We are infected with the sinful nature of Adam from birth. All of us have fallen short of God's perfect standard of holiness (Romans 3:23). From the very beginning, the cost of sin has been death (Genesis 2:16-17). Sin is such a serious offense to God that He will always judge it, and His judgment demands death. Do you grasp the gravity of sin? Can you fathom that even seemingly good people are sinners by nature? If so, who among us has any hope, any chance of heaven or pleasing God in any way? None of us. Not a single one of us.

But God....

God demonstrated His love for us, not when we became good or practiced religion or paid penitence. Rather He demonstrated His love for us while we were still sinners

(Romans 5:8). Dear one, God's love is demonstrated to us through His mercy and His grace. The Apostle Paul writes, *"But God being rich in mercy, because of His great love with which He loves us, even when we were dead in our transgressions, made us alive together with Christ (by grace you have been saved)"* (Ephesians 2:4-5). In mercy, God compassionately withholds the judgment we deserve for our sin. In grace, He gives us what we do not deserve, the free gift of salvation through Jesus Christ.

This is the gospel. We deserve judgment and death, but Jesus took our place. Jesus is God's sacrificial lamb. Jesus is the mercy seat. All those years ago, God accepted sacrifices of lambs and goats and bulls. He accepted the blood of animals to temporarily cover the sin of His people. In His perfect plan and timing, God Himself has provided a better sacrifice. A perfect sacrifice. He has given His perfect son Jesus, and His blood cleanses us from all sin—once and for all (Hebrews 10:10-18).

Do you see the great cost of God's compassion for us? When we have a clear understanding of God's holiness and the gravity of sin, mercy becomes shocking and grace overwhelming. His mercy has been at work from the beginning. It is still at work through Jesus Christ, changing us, redeeming us, compelling us to new life.

Jesus' final statement to the woman *go your way; and from now on, sin no more* is not a side note or suggestion. In essence, Jesus is saying, "Mercy makes a difference. Live in a way that demonstrates you have experienced God's mercy." He is forgiving but He is also redeeming. To *redeem* means to buy back and make new. While He forgives her sin, He also lifts her out of the shame of her sin. She isn't to hide in shame for the rest of her life. Neither is she to continually look back and be paralyzed by guilt. Jesus tells her to live!

Shame is the unforeseen consequence of sin. It is a weapon in the arsenal of our enemy, Satan. We are often tempted to sin, but when we succumb to the temptation, the tempter becomes the accuser. His accusations against us always bring shame. Listen carefully. The enemy wants to keep us in the shame. Why? Because shame will cause us to turn away from God. Shame will put a resistance in our hearts against the Word of God and the people of God. It brings our sin into laser focus while blurring the work of grace in our lives. Shame worms its way into our soul, casting doubt on every promise God has given and every blessing God has provided through Christ. Sadly, if shame is left to its own devises, it can draw us back into the very sin that caused the shame in the first place.

Jesus came to pardon our sin and shatter the shame that accompanies it. This is not glib, lighthearted, easy theology. There are often consequences to sin that God does not reverse. Sin is harmful to both the sinner and to others. For the woman in John 8, there are undoubtedly relationships that are either irreparably destroyed or deeply damaged by her sin. Her own reputation must be rebuilt over time as those who love her learn to trust her. Consequences may seem insurmountable and overwhelming…

But God…

Because God's mercies are new every day, He redeems even the consequences of our sin for our good and His glory. His compassion never fails. His goodness never ends. Not only has the Lord paid the price for sin, but He is faithful to make all things new (2 Corinthians 5:17).

Oh, I have made choices in my life with severe consequences attached. Often, I am tempted to look back at my sin and shortsighted decisions, and in looking back relive the heat of shame. *But God...*reminds me the only reason to look back is to see His mercy and grace at work in my life. For all of us, the Lord is able to do a new and redeeming work within us. He makes a road in our wilderness and a river in our desert. Because of His unfailing love, He makes all things new. Our response is to receive His gift of mercy and forgiveness and, like the woman caught in adultery, *go our way and sin no more.*

Do not call to mind the former things or ponder things of the past. Behold I will do something new, now it will spring forth; will you not be aware of it? I will even make a roadway in the wilderness, rivers in the desert. (Isaiah 43:18-19)

Perhaps one of the most compelling accounts of compassion is found in Luke 15. We have come to know it as the story of the prodigal son. Pastor and author Timothy Keller explains that the word *prodigal* means "to spend until you have nothing left; recklessly spendthrift." Traditionally, we have applied that definition to the wayward son who defies his father and squanders his inheritance. But Timothy Keller aptly applies the word *prodigal* to the father in the story, the father who represents God.

"The father's welcome to the repentant son was literally reckless, because he refused to 'reckon' or count his sins against him or demand repayment. ...Jesus is showing us the God of Great Expenditure, who is nothing if not prodigal toward us, His children" (Timothy J Keller, *The Prodigal God*).

When I read Jesus' parable of the returning son and the prodigal father, I can rarely contain my tears. The mercy of the

Father overwhelms me. It takes my breath away. It humbles me and yet compels me to live out the new life He offers. For the woman caught in adultery, for the wayward son, for you, and for me, God the Father pours out His love and compassion on us…and it changes everything.

When (the son) finally came to his senses, he said to himself, "At home even the hired servants have food enough to spare and here I am dying of hunger! I will go home to my father and say, 'Father, I have sinned against both heaven and you, and I am no longer worthy of being called your son. Please take me on as a hired servant.'" So, he returned home to his father.

And while he was still a long way off, the father saw him coming. Filled with love and compassion, he ran to his son, embraced him and kissed him.

His son said to him, "Father, I have sinned against heaven and you, and I am no longer worthy of being called your son."

But his father said to the servants, "Quick! Bring the finest robe in the house and put it on him. Get a ring for his finger and sandals for his feet. And kill the calf we have been fattening. We must celebrate with a feast, for this son of mine was dead and has now returned to life. He was lost, and now he is found." (Luke 15:17-22 NLT)

Mercy Applied to Sorrow and Suffering

God's mercy is ongoing in our lives. Certainly, we experience mercy (and grace) for salvation, but we also experience His deep compassion in the sorrows and suffering we are sure to encounter in this life. Remember, God's mercy is not sympathy or pity. His mercy is active compassion moving to meet our needs. He does not respond to us haphazardly. He is not patching things up for us. His mercy is always purposeful. It is redemptive, making all things new for His purpose and His glory.

The gospels give dozens of accounts of Jesus' kindness and mercy extended to people who are experiencing sorrow or suffering. His reputation for compassion is the overwhelming draw for the crowds who sought Him. In fact, *"Have mercy on me"* is the most often made request of Jesus in the Gospels... and Jesus never said *no*. A cry for mercy was always met with compassion. It still is.

The Gospel of Luke presents an account that makes me smile every time I read it. Maybe I smile because I love stories and Luke's words ignite a compelling scene in my mind. Envision with me the unfolding events of Luke 18:35-43.

At this point in Jesus' ministry, the crowd has become a constant presence. His reputation as a compassionate healer and authoritative teacher has ignited the grapevine of communication, drawing a diverse multitude of sceptics, seekers, and believers. The eclectic crowd surrounds Jesus as He approaches the city of Jericho. Excited chatter and a cloud of road dust announce His coming.

Just outside the city, beggars line the road anticipating the normal foot traffic of an active day. They are people with overwhelming needs, relentlessly asking strangers for alms or assistance. Most of society ignores them. Even the passersby who contribute a coin or two certainly avoid eye contact. Afterall, heaven only knows what diseases the beggars carry or the number of lice they house. I can imagine fretful mothers pulling their children close and admonishing them as they walk past the line of beggars, "Children, don't look at them and for goodness' sake, don't touch them!" Yes, beggars are a hopeless lot…until this day when Jesus passes by.

Bartimaeus is a blind beggar. Years of sitting alongside the dusty road, shouting over the other beggars has become a way of life and survival. When he hears the excited chatter of the crowd, it occurs to him that a rich man or a generous man could be passing by—one who might deposit liberally into his beggar's cup. His curiosity and his desperation demand to know what the excitement is about. Perhaps to shut him up, someone tells Bartimaeus that Jesus of Nazareth is passing by.

An ever-so-slight pause momentarily silences the beggar. Pieces of information and roadway news coupled with teachings from his childhood of a coming Messiah stir up a hope in Bartimaeus that has laid dormant for decades. Bartimaeus knows he cannot help himself or change his own circumstances. He understands his only hope would have to come from outside of himself. That hope is passing by. With desperate grit, he pushes his way into the road, shamelessly, tenaciously, repeatedly crying out, *"Son of David, have mercy on me!"*

And Jesus stops.

Jesus commands that the beggar be brought near (vs 40). It is an authoritative request. The Bible says those who are leading the impromptu procession into Jericho are sternly shushing Bartimaeus. I wonder who was leading the way. Perhaps it was Jesus' disciples clearing a path, protecting their teacher, thinking they knew what was best in the situation. But

Jesus commands something different. His command means that someone would have to get close enough to smell the beggar, to see the glassy blind eyes, and in obedience to the Teacher, physically touch Bartimaeus and bring him to Jesus. Compassion suddenly becomes uncomfortable for everyone except Jesus and Bartimaeus.

And when Bartimaeus came near, Jesus questioned him, "What do you want me to do for you?"

Jesus hears the unspecified cry for mercy, but in this up-close and personal conversation, Jesus gives Bartimaeus an opportunity to verbalize a specific request. Like so many others who have lived long years on the edge of desperate, Bartimaeus wants the obvious. He wants Jesus to heal his eyes. Jesus, however, is interested in far more.

There is always greater purpose in God's mercy than simply fixing the obviously broken things in our lives. In fact, there are times when God does not heal the sickness or relieve the suffering or change the circumstances. Where is God's compassion in those instances? Is He deaf to our cry for mercy? Or is He doing something beyond the obvious?

That day, Jesus gives Bartimaeus sight and qualifies the healing with a phrase that often trips us up. *"...your faith has made you well."* Did Bartimaeus believe hard enough? Ask loud enough? Claim his healing with confidence? The answer to all these questions is NO!

Notice that blind Bartimaeus cries out to the *Son of David* for mercy. The title *Son of David* is an often-used designation for God's Messiah. Based on 2 Samuel 7, the Jews acknowledged that God's Messiah would come from King

David's lineage. In Matthew's gospel, great care is taken to show the reader that Jesus is indeed the Messiah, coming from the ancestral line of David. For Bartimaeus to cry out for the Son of David indicates that God had given the blind beggar a glimmer of spiritual insight to discern who Jesus was.

Bartimaeus acts on the truth God has revealed to him. He responds in faith to the tiny kernel of truth he possesses. Bartimaeus certainly doesn't fully understood everything about Jesus, but he acts on the mustard seed of faith he has. In faith, he cries for mercy. It is not the bigness of his faith or the decibel level of his cry or the boldness of any claim that catches Jesus' attention. It was the direction of his faith— the person in whom he has put his faith that made all the difference. It is not big faith or loud faith or dramatic faith but rightly placed faith that pleases God. Bartimaeus believes Jesus is the Messiah. He acts on the truth by humbly crying out. And Jesus responds to Bartimaeus' faith.

When you and I are suffering, when we are hurting, when we are desperate for God's intervention in our lives, in faith we can turn to Christ. The Lord is not asking for perfectly mature faith. He desires rightly placed faith. Faith requires that we come to the end of ourselves and our own resources. It requires that we lay down our well-thought-out plans. It requires that we bring our brokenhearted request with open hands to the Son of David, Jesus the Messiah. Why did Jesus always respond to the often-made cry for mercy? Because *a cry for mercy is a cry of faith.* The request for mercy is acknowledging a powerlessness within us to resolve the problem, heal the condition, or relieve the suffering. *Have mercy on me* is a verbal surrender to the compassion of Christ, trusting Him to meet our greatest need.

I realize as I type these words that many of you are

suffering with difficult and desperate circumstances. I do not want to give the impression that saying the words *have mercy on me* is the magical formula to strong-arm God into giving us what we want. In fact, there are times when God does not relieve our suffering or change our circumstances (2 Corinthians 12:8-10). So where is God's mercy during sorrow and suffering? Let's go back to Luke's account of Bartimaeus. If we miss the last verse in the story, we miss the purpose of God's mercy altogether.

And immediately he received his sight, and began following Him, glorifying God; and when all the people saw it, they gave praise to God. (Luke 18:43)

There was something greater at stake for Bartimaeus—his soul. In compassion, Jesus allows the beggar to ask for the obvious, knowing all along Bartimaeus needs much more. Bartimaeus needs a relationship with Christ. He needs a changed life more than he needs changed eyes. With great mercy—Jesus gives him both.

The blind beggar was changed that day along the dusty road to Jericho. Not only did he gain his sight, but he followed Jesus, giving God the glory. Bartimaeus had an encounter with the Savior. Like the woman caught in adultery, like Moses, like Jairus, and like every person who has been changed by Christ…life would never be the same. And other people notice.

The crowd who had either shushed or ignored Bartimaeus now glorified God with him. Yes, God gave Bartimaeus sight, but He also brought Bartimaeus into a new relationship with the Son of David, the Messiah. The ripple effect of God's work in Bartimaeus is that many saw and believed. Jesus had more in mind for God's glory and God's kingdom than Bartimaeus could fathom. God still works that way.

When we are living on the edge of desperate, it is easy to feel as if God has forsaken us or that somehow His mercy has dried up. God's compassion, however, is always at work, moving to meet our greatest need. Dear one, our greatest need is not relief from physical suffering or even a new set of circumstances. Our greatest need is to know God through Jesus Christ. Even for the believer in Christ, our greatest need is to know Him more. Certainly, we have the Lord in full, and we will spend our entire lives gaining an ever-deepening knowledge of Christ.

So, what about pain and suffering and blindness and…? God is near to the brokenhearted. He hears the cries of His people. His ears are not deaf to our pleas for mercy and relief. The Lord, in mercy, responds to us with compassion. He never says no to a cry for mercy. Our responsibility is to trust His heart, even when His response seems to be different from what we asked.

As I write these words, I am not spouting platitudes from a place of little or no suffering. I have been a young widow, a cancer patient, a struggling mom and wife. I have pleaded for God's mercy for relief from issues that have plagued me for years. Most recently, my husband Allen has been diagnosed with a severe health condition. We have cried out for God's mercy, and true to His Word, the Lord's mercy is new every day.

While Allen's health condition remains, we sense the Lord's presence, His peace, His goodness. We have experienced great kindness from doctors, technicians, and nurses. We have been loved well by friends and family, watching relationships strengthened through the very adversity we would gladly release. These blessings are not substitutes for His mercy. They *are* His mercy.

Oh, precious reader, God hears your cry for mercy. When you feel as if you cannot live another moment on the edge of desperate, He is actively at work in your circumstances. He is doing more than meeting the obvious needs which we often perceive as the only needs. Knowing Christ deeply and intimately is our greatest need. If He does not immediately relieve the suffering in our lives, He is still there in the middle of the suffering. His mercy is present even as His goodness and our suffering coexist.

Katherine Wolf is a writer and speaker. Her story is riddled with suffering and loss. As a twenty-six-year-old young woman with a wonderful husband and brand-new baby, Katherine suffered a massive brainstem stroke. She was given little hope of survival, yet miraculously she survived. Her life, however, has been changed forever. Katherine suffers daily from the effects of the stoke, but in her daily suffering, she brings hope to others. In her recent book *Treasures in the Dark*, she writes,

I'm training myself to celebrate rather than just tolerate my broken brain and body because they didn't ruin my perfect life; they gave me the gift of a good/hard life. Because my body has suffered, my soul has flourished. Because my health and wellness failed me in every material way, my life embodies hope. Because I live in the fallible human body, I can know Jesus a little better. (90)

Perhaps physical suffering is not what elicits your cry for mercy; perhaps it is sorrow. Sorrows usually come from loss, regret, or past experiences which have ongoing effects. For me, it seems life's greatest sorrows are attached to relationships, and most often to the people I love most. Sorrows are a heaviness, a weighty burden we carry in the most tender and vulnerable part of our souls.

While Jesus is ever present in our suffering, He is equally present in our sorrows. He understands the burdens we carry and the losses we grieve because He has walked through sorrow too. In fact, He is described as a man of sorrows and acquainted with grief…the only one qualified to bear our grief and carry our sorrow (Isaiah 53:3-4). Jesus never turns away from the sorrows of His people. In mercy, He carries those sorrows.

The psalms are filled with cries for mercy and help in sorrowful times. Psalm 3 is written by King David during a terrifying and heartbreaking crisis. He is fleeing Jerusalem because his son Absalom is attempting to usurp the throne. Even though Absalom has murder and deceit in his heart, David is filled with sorrow over his rebellious son. In the sorrowful circumstances, David turns to the Lord with confidence. He has experienced the goodness and kindness of the Lord in days past, and so in the tumultuous days of fleeing, David writes,

Thou, O Lord are a shield about me, my glory, and the One who lifts my head. (Psalm 3:3)

In the sorrowful days, His mercy reaches into our pit of sadness—and lifts our head to see the hope of Christ. He adjusts our focus. With great tenderness, He reminds us of His goodness, His provision, and His love. He will not let us go.

He will not abandon us in our sorrows. Our responsibility is to keep our eyes on Him, even through the tears.

In Psalm 23, David also reminds us that the Lord is a good and all-sufficient Shepherd. He leads us through the dark valleys of difficult circumstances. He may not take us around the dark valley or over it or even provide an immediate exit from it, but He leads the way through it—at His pace and with His merciful care guarding us all along the way. David concludes Psalm 23 with a joyful picture of God's goodness and mercy following us all the days of our lives. Again, our focus is on the One leading the way and lifting our heads, confident that His mercy and goodness are always close.

We began this chapter with a woman caught in adultery. She encounters mercy instead of condemnation when Jesus pardons her sin and frees her from shame. Bartimaeus cries out for mercy in his suffering and despair. Jesus extends mercy even greater and more far-reaching than a physical healing. Jesus gives the blind man sight, but He also gives new life. In the Psalms, David records his cries for help and mercy. God always responds with lovingkindness—not because David is so special, but because God is so faithful.

Do you see it? Mercy is always waiting and always available because that is who God is. We simply must be willing to receive it. It's interesting to note that God is merciful whether we ask for His mercy or not. The woman in John 8 did not come asking for mercy, but Jesus gave it anyway. With a humble heart, the woman had to receive His mercy and live accordingly.

Can you look back and see the mercy of God at work in your life? Do you understand His mercy and grace are the key elements in securing your relationship with Him? Can you look back at the dark valleys of life and see His care and His tender provision? Have you sensed His comfort in the sorrowful days? Has He ever lifted your head, refocusing your tear-filled eyes on His faithfulness, even while the difficulties remain?

If you answer yes to any of these questions, you have experienced His lovingkindness…yes, the mercy of God. In receiving His mercy, we are called and qualified to demonstrate mercy to others.

Mercy Applied to Daily Living

Jesus' Sermon on the Mount reminds us that mercy has a cyclical pattern. Those who give mercy also receive mercy (Matthew 5:7). Elsewhere, we are reminded that those who have received mercy must demonstrate mercy (Luke 6:36). Mercy generously flows from God the Father to His people. His people become vessels of mercy, both receiving God's mercy as well as pouring out mercy to others.

When we practice mercy, we are concerned about the needs of others and act to relieve their suffering. Extending mercy, however, requires more than just a sweet attitude. It requires the Holy Spirit living within us, empowering us for right living. Truthfully, many people do not deserve our mercy. But consider this—neither do we deserve mercy. Because of God's great love, demonstrated through mercy and grace, He saved us while we were enemies of God (Romans 5:8-10). We have received undeserved mercy, and we are told to extend it to others. While we cannot save a person, the Holy Spirit will use our acts of mercy to draw a lost person to Christ. God's mercy always has redemption at the heart of it.

A familiar story in Luke's gospel gives us God's perspective about mercy. Jesus tells the story of a merciful

Samaritan—a shocking plot twist for the Jews who were listening. Actually, the Jews and the Samaritans had a mutual disdain for one another. The animosity went back centuries. The Jews hated the Samaritans for being apostate, half-breed Jews (1 Kings 12:16-33, 2 Kings 17:6-23). The Samaritans hated the Jews for their smoldering condescension and relentless oppression. So when Jesus tells a story about mercy within the context of ongoing racial and religious hatred, everyone tuned in to listen—especially the self-righteous lawyer who started the entire conversation.

Jesus is teaching in the town of Capernaum, and as usual, a diverse crowd has gathered to hear Him. Jesus pauses just long enough for a lawyer, one skilled in the Jewish law, to stand and ask Jesus a question. It seems the lawyer thinks highly of himself. His question is prideful. Paraphrased, he asks, "What must I do to have eternal life, since I already know and obey the Law thoroughly?" I think Jesus must have given an inner eye roll, but with patience He engages the lawyer with questions of His own. "What is written in the Law? How do you interpret it?" The lawyer smiles and gladly quotes from Leviticus and Deuteronomy basically saying to love God and to love your neighbor. Jesus nods, knowing the man has no real understanding of what he is spouting or to whom he is speaking. Jesus responds, "Yes, that is true. Now go do it." But again, the lawyer wants to prove he is perfectly righteous in obeying the Law. Looking for approval, he asks, "Who is my neighbor?"

Do you see it? The lawyer is putting limits on compassion. To him, loving his neighbor is a dutiful exercise in rulekeeping. He only wants to dispense kindness to the right people and to the right degree—no more, no less—so that the Law is perfectly, but not extravagantly, fulfilled. Jesus turns to the listening crowd and tells a story that will expand their understanding of mercy far beyond the limits of religion. His story will also shatter the lawyer's interpretation of the Mosaic Law.

And Jesus replied and said, "A certain man was going down from Jerusalem to Jericho; and he fell among robbers, and they stripped him and beat him, and went off leaving him half dead." (Luke 10:30)

Because Jesus does not qualify the race or religion of the victim, everyone in the Jewish crowd knows the unfortunate man is Jewish. As Jesus continues the story, the crowd is appalled but not surprised that first a Jewish priest and later a Jewish Levite do not stop to give aid. In fact, the two highly religious men cross to the other side of the road, too busy, too afraid, or too uncaring to even look in the direction of their dying countryman.

Completely engrossed in the story, the crowd is silent while Jesus continues.

A third man, a Samaritan, comes upon the bloody scene. He sees the dying, naked, beaten Jewish man—and the apostate, half-breed from Samaria has compassion on his enemy.

In stunned disbelief, the listening crowd (and the lawyer) gasp. But Jesus isn't finished.

The Samaritan cleans and binds the man's wounds. He forfeits his own comfort by putting the injured Jew on his donkey. He takes the half-dead victim to an inn and stays to care for him. The next day, the Samaritan pays the innkeeper to continue caring for the man, promising to repay the innkeeper for any additional charges. The Samaritan leaves the injured man in good hands, but he leaves with no applause, no thanks, and no special recognition for his kindness.

I can imagine the listening audience with perplexed expressions on their faces and exploding questions in their minds. Why would a Samaritan show kindness to a Jew? Other than being desperate and possibly unconscious, why would a Jew accept kindness from an unclean Samaritan? The lawyer is scrolling through his memory searching for laws and ordinances that apply to the unusual story, but none come to mind. Jesus is stretching everyone's understanding of mercy to the breaking point. He drives home the lesson as He turns to the lawyer and asks,

"Which of these three do you think proved to be a neighbor to the man who fell into the robbers' hands?" (Luke 10:36)

While the answer is obvious, speaking it must feel like sand in the lawyer's throat. *"The one who showed mercy toward him."* Truth has hit its mark, and hopefully it is breaking through the years of legalism. Jesus nods in agreement and says, *"Go and do the same."*

On more than one occasion, Jesus rebuked the religious leaders for being exact with the Law but lacking in mercy. Skillfully, He has brought the lawyer to a fresh understanding of mercy through a story that speaks to us as well. Jesus' final words to the lawyer are not a suggestion to the lawyer or to us. *"Go and do the same"* is a command to demonstrate mercy outside our comfort zone—to be vessels of mercy in a world that doesn't think like us or look like us or act like us. We are told to pour out the love of Christ on a thirsty, wounded population who may reject us or even persecute us.

While indeed the world is our neighbor, we are also commanded to show mercy to the people closest to us. The Apostle Paul writes, *"And be kind to one another, tender-hearted, forgiving each other, just as God in Christ has also forgiven you"* (Ephesians 4:32). Compassion begins at home with the very ones who have the greatest ability to wound us. When we are hurt by those we love or by people who are supposed to care for us, resentment and unforgiveness can quickly take root. Paul warns us to put away all the anger and bitterness (Ephesians 4:31). If we know Christ, we have been made new. God's mercy has made a difference in us, and we must allow it to make a difference in our relationships as well.

Often mercy must be accompanied by forgiveness. Remember the woman caught in adultery? Jesus did not ignore her sin. Instead, He pardoned her sin. You and I cannot pardon sin. We cannot remove sin from someone's life, but we can extend forgiveness toward those who have wounded us. Forgiving allows us to release the hurt to the Lord, and also releases the offending person to the Lord. We trust God to deal with our offender and to deal with our hurt as well.

I stated earlier that mercy operates in a cycle. We receive mercy from God, and we demonstrate mercy to others. When mercy and forgiveness are regularly exercised, our daily living honors God. Certainly, mercy is not sappy tolerance. Neither is it a doormat mentality void of discernment. Jesus never sacrificed truth for mercy. He exercised both in perfect unity. Likewise, the mercy we offer to others must always operate in truth and love. The Holy Spirit uses the Word of God to equip us and teach us how to do both.

In closing this chapter, there can be no doubt that God's mercy is transformational. It changes everyone it touches—

the woman caught in adultery, the wayward son, Bartimaeus, the psalmist, and perhaps even the questioning lawyer. Oh, how mercy has changed me too. While circumstances remain challenging, God's mercies are new each day. So, with great compassion and humility, allow me to ask a few questions.

Have you experienced God's mercy? Do you understand that all of us deserve judgment, but God chose to offer mercy instead? Will you humbly receive the mercy He is offering? Has suffering and sorrow temporarily blinded you to His goodness? Will you allow His merciful hands to lift your head and open your eyes to see His compassion?

The edge of desperate can feel like a dry and weary land, void of mercy. Sin, shame, suffering, and sorrow feel like cracked and brittle bricks lining every path. But God is at work. His mercies are new every day. He is paving a new road with His goodness and His faithfulness. He is creating rivers of mercy that redeem and refresh. Because of Christ, mercy flows, mercy redeems, and mercy transforms. Mercy for you. Mercy for me.

Discussion Questions
Desperate for Mercy

1. Define or describe mercy in your own words. Describe what mercy is not.

2. How does Jesus demonstrate mercy to the adulterous woman in John 8? When she receives God's mercy, how will her life be different?

3. Read the Apostle Paul's words in Ephesians 2:4-5 and discuss how God's mercy is linked to God's grace in our lives.

4. Jesus responded to Bartimaeus' cry, *"Son of David, have mercy on me!"* (Luke18:38). Did Jesus respond to the depth of Bartimaeus' faith? Or did Jesus respond to the placement or direction of Bartimaeus' faith? Discuss the difference.

5. Jennifer writes, *"Have mercy on me* is a verbal surrender to the compassion of Christ, trusting Him to meet our greatest need." What is every person's greatest need? Read John 3:16, John 10:10, John 12:46, and 2 Corinthians 5:17.

6. Read 2 Corinthians 12:8-10. Have you ever experienced God's mercy even when suffering remains? Would you share how you have seen God's mercy working in your life? Do you agree with David in Psalm 23:6, that God's mercy follows us all the days of our life?

7. Mercy has a cyclical pattern. As we receive mercy, we become vessels to extend mercy. Would you share an example of how you have demonstrated mercy to someone else?

7

DESPERATE
For Community
Luke 8:43-48

"But as He went..." Do you remember these
words from Luke 8:42? We started this book with a desperate
man named Jairus. His little girl is dying and Jairus pleads
with Jesus to come to his house and heal his daughter. Jesus
responds to Jairus' urgent request. In spite of the crushing
crowd, Jesus adjusts His route and heads toward the home of
Jairus.

But as He went, something extraordinary happens. The
story of Jairus is interrupted by an anonymous woman, a
desperate woman. For six verses, Jesus puts Jairus on hold, and
He deals with a woman who is not only sick but also scorned
and ostracized. Her story is not simply another healing. Her
story is one of redemption and restoration. It speaks to us

across the centuries of God's love for us and our God-designed need for community.

The Woman's Condition

The anonymous woman has been hemorrhaging for twelve years. Her condition is a heavy and constant flow of blood—an ongoing menstrual cycle or physical illness. Certainly, twelve years of heavy bleeding would cause anemia, pain, discomfort, and exhaustion. The Gospel of Mark says she has suffered much at the hands of physicians, spending everything she has, looking for a cure. Nothing helps. In fact, she gets worse (Mark 5:26).

When Scripture says she suffered much, it is referring to more than physical pain. Ancient remedies were often more painful and humiliating than the condition. Having suffered for so long, she is at the end of her rope. The lack of help and hope gives way to emotional and mental despair. Poverty and isolation accentuate every kind of pain. This bleeding woman is not just sick. She is utterly desperate.

The Law of Moses helps us better understand her plight. Keep in mind, everything about the Old Testament points us to the New Testament. Also remember the bleeding woman is Jewish, living in or around the Jewish city of Capernaum. In Jesus day, the purity of the Mosaic Law has been diluted, but it still dictates the lives of the Jewish people. Strict adherence to religious laws is overseen by the religious leaders—often without mercy.

Throughout Scripture, blood always holds great meaning and importance. *For the life of the flesh is in the blood...for it is the blood by reason of the life that makes atonement* (Leviticus 17:11). From the beginning, blood has been shed to cover sin.

When Adam and Eve sinned, God used the skin of an animal to cover the nakedness of the rebellious couple. The animal's blood was shed and its life given to provide that covering (Genesis 2:16-17, 3:21). Later, God gave Israel the sacrificial system whereby an animal was sacrificed. The shed blood of the animal served as a covering over the sins of the people, purging their sin and purifying them before God.

Because blood is a holy and powerful symbol of God's provision for the cleansing of sin, the Israelites were given many laws concerning blood. Any contact with blood rendered a person ceremonially unclean. The contaminated person was temporarily excluded from worship and isolated from other Israelites. Cleansing required bathing and washing one's clothes. Afterwards, the unclean person would remain separated from people, though not scorned by them, until the day passed and evening arrived. Reuniting with family and friends at the end of the day would be a joyful time of restoration.

God's laws were designed to continually remind His people of their relationship with a Holy God. Everything about their daily lives pointed them toward the redemptive heart of God. *Everything.* Even a woman's monthly menstrual cycle.

Whenever a woman has her menstrual period, she will be ceremonially unclean for seven days. Anyone who touches her during that time will be unclean until evening. Anything on which the woman lies or sits during the time of her period will be unclean. If any of you touch her bed , you must wash your clothes and bathe yourself in water, and you will remain unclean until evening. If you touch any object she has sat on, you must wash your clothes and bathe yourself in water, and you will remain unclean until evening. This includes her bed or any other object she has sat on; you will be unclean until evening. If a man has sexual intercourse with her and her blood touches him, her menstrual impurity will be transmitted to him. He will remain unclean for seven days, and any bed on which he lies will be unclean. (Leviticus 15:19-24 NLT)

An uninformed reading of Leviticus 15 might leave us thinking that God views a woman's cycle as dirty or shameful. We would be wrong. In fact, in the Old Testament God uses a woman's menstrual cycle as a beautiful illustration of His cleansing and purging from sin. Physically, her body is being cleansed, getting rid of what is no longer needed. Spiritually, her menstruating body is illustrating God's cleansing from sin with blood (Leviticus 16).

The ancient Jewish family participates in the illustration— every month. For a Jewish woman, it is a time to teach her children about God's atonement. Her flow of blood is a reminder for the entire family that Holy God purges and purifies. Avoiding any place she sleeps or sits is not mean-spirited. Avoidance is part of the illustration, reminding God's people that sin effects everyone it touches. The woman temporarily lives in another part of the house, reminding her family that sin is serious and separates people from God. Her separation also illustrates that God will not allow His people to cohabit with sin. The menstruating woman is a beautiful picture of God's atonement, cleansing His people and making them pure through the washing of blood.

The ongoing condition of the woman in Luke 8 is also addressed in the Mosaic Law. Leviticus 15:25-28 states that any woman who bleeds for many days that are not part of her monthly cycle is considered ceremonially unclean for as long as she bleeds. All the restrictions and requirements that pertain to a woman and her family during the natural menstrual cycle also pertain to a woman who is discharging blood at any other time (Leviticus 15:25-28).

Dear reader, God's laws in the Old Testament were never meant to demean or ridicule anyone. If a person was rendered ceremonially unclean for any reason, it did not give other people permission to mistreat, abuse, or neglect the person. God required that kindness and love always be shown toward fellow Israelites (Leviticus 19:9-18). Furthermore, being ceremonial unclean never negated God's covenant with a person, although, for a season, it separated the person from fellowship with others and public worship of God.

The Mosaic Law had a dual purpose. Many of God's laws were meant to keep His people safe. Dietary laws, laws about diseases, and some of the sundry laws all had health benefits for the community. At the same time, His laws directed His people to always and in everything remember His matchless holiness and His great love for them. The Law was a signpost directing His people to live holy lives, distinctly different from the nations around them. Every law that God gave was preparing their hearts for Christ.

For Christians, God's atoning work through the shed blood of Christ is not an illustration. It is God's mighty work of salvation foreshadowed long ago. Jesus Christ is the perfect and permanent sacrifice, cleansing us from sin and making us new. The great cost of God's forgiveness compels us to live holy lives, freed eternally from the penalty of sin and freed daily to live in victory over sin. For the New Testament believer, every Old Testament Law has been perfectly fulfilled in Christ.

By the time Jesus begins His earthly ministry, over six hundred additional laws had been added to the Mosaic Law. Over the centuries the Law had been needlessly expanded and distorted. Keeping the law, both God's and man's additions to the Law, became more important than mercy. Religion became more important than people. The bleeding woman in Capernaum is not a beautiful picture of atonement. She is a picture of suffering not only from an illness but also from rigid and unmerciful legalism. Jesus breaks through the legalism. In dealing with the bleeding woman, He is not ignoring the Law of God. In mercy, He is fulfilling it.

What does the Law, the added laws, and the cultural Jewish mindset mean for the woman who has been bleeding for twelve years? It means for twelve years she has not felt the touch of another person. She has not been hugged or caressed. She has not held a child or wiped a baby's tears. She has not eaten a meal with friends or laughed with other women. She cannot maintain or develop meaningful relationships. She cannot go to the market place to buy food lest she brush against someone or touch their clothes accidently rendering that person unclean. She has no job, no way to earn a living. She has been alone every Sabbath and forbidden to participate in religious feasts and festivals. For twelve years, she has been prohibited from publicly worshiping God.

This desperate bleeding woman has been completely cut off from society. She has no connection to the people around her and seemingly no connection to God. Indeed, her physical condition is painful, but the isolation is crushing. Of all the people I have included in this book, my heart aches the most for her. She does not live on the edge of desperate. She lives in the very center of it, and she has lived there for twelve long years.

For some of us, this entire subject of a bleeding woman may feel uncomfortable. However, if we do not understand the Old Testament teaching and the cultural context surrounding the woman's condition, we will never grasp the magnificent impact of her healing.

The Woman's Restoration

Over the centuries, the six hundred additional laws were also accompanied by the Jewish oral law. Like the additional laws, the oral law was not divinely inspired. It was the extra writings of rabbis which were taught and followed with the same vigor as the Mosaic Law. The oral law stated that when the Messiah came, a sick person could touch the hem, most likely the prayer tassel, of His outer garment and be healed.

When Jesus comes to Capernaum, He brings an atmosphere of excitement. He also brings expectancy and hope—especially for the sick or suffering. The crowds have been waiting for Him to return to the area. They have already heard His teaching and seen the miracles so their buzzing excitement cannot be quieted.

Perhaps from a hidden place, the bleeding woman overhears the news that Jesus is coming. Stories of healing circulate through the streets every time Jesus visits Capernaum. Those stories ignite memories from her childhood. From her youth, she has been taught that a sick person could be healed by God's Messiah just by touching His outer garment. In her mind, the stories of healing and the oral teaching about a Messiah begin to come together. Truth begins to dawn. Jesus of Nazareth is the Messiah.

For the first time in twelve years, hope begins to stir within her. If only she could get close enough to touch the hem of His garment. If only she could slip through the crowd unnoticed. If only she could reach out her hand and ever so slightly graze her fingers across the prayer tassel…she would be healed.

Cloaked and hiding in the shadows, she waits for the perfect opportunity to move through the crowd toward Jesus. When the people are distracted, when Jesus is not looking, when some other desperate person captures center stage…then she will make her move. Jairus gives the bleeding woman the opportunity she needs. While all eyes are on this important man prostrating himself in the dust, pleading for his dying daughter, the bleeding woman presses in…and touches the hem of Jesus' garment.

Immediately, the bleeding stops. She knows she has received the healing she came for—but if they see her, the crowd won't understand or care. Oh, if she can slip away unnoticed, she can save herself the public shame of being discovered. Instead, Jesus suddenly stops and the parade of people around Him stops as well. *Who touched me?* Jesus asks. Of course, Peter is the first to speak, chiding the Lord for asking such a ridiculous question. *Everyone is touching you, Master!* Jesus insists, however, that someone touched Him specifically—differently than the pressing crowd.

Is there any doubt that sovereign, omniscient, Almighty God knew exactly who touched Him and why she touched Him? He knew every detail of her miserable life. He chose the route to Jairus' house knowing she was in the shadows. So why does He ask, as if surprised, *"Who touched Me?"*

Even though the woman wants to slip away and remain anonymous, Jesus has a greater purpose. He is intentional in everything He does. No one can secretly steal a healing. He does not want superstition to distort His ministry. No hint

of touching the talisman, rubbing the rabbit's foot, placing
a hand on the television screen, or sprinkling the fairy dust
will distract from His authority. While the woman only wants
an anonymous healing, Jesus wants more for her than she
ever imagined. He wants to give her an abundant life. In the
presence of the entire community, and perhaps even in the
presence of her estranged family, Jesus publicly calls attention
to her.

*And when the woman saw that she had not escaped notice, she
came trembling and fell down before Him, and declared in the
presence of all the people the reason why she had touched Him,
and how she had been immediately healed.* (Luke 8:47)

Surely, when the crowd catches a glimpse of her, they
recognize her and quickly move away disgusted yet intrigued.
Someone probably yells a warning of *unclean*. She cannot
escape the public shame, but neither can she escape the look
of mercy in Jesus' eyes. Likewise, she can't ignore the healing
in her body. Trembling, she follows the example of Jairus and
falls before Jesus. The dust of desperation chokes her as she
tearfully tries to explain.

"Master, I have been sick and unclean for twelve years.
No one is allowed to touch me or be near me. As a child, I
was taught that one day God's Messiah would come, and the
sick could be healed by touching His outer garment while He
passed by. I believe you are the Messiah. I know you are the
Messiah. I touched the edge of your garment, Lord, and I am
healed."

Jesus knows every indignation she has suffered. He
understands that heartache and loneliness have been her

constant companions. He is well aware of her physical pain as well as her mental anguish. Compassion spills from His eyes as He addresses her with the tenderness of a loving father.

And He said to her, "Daughter, your faith has made you well; go in peace." (Luke 8:48)

While Jesus' words to her are simple and succinct, His words bring new life. He speaks to her the same phrase He has spoken to so many others—*your faith has made you well.* Remember, Jesus is not commending her for the depth of her faith. He is commending her for the direction of her faith. Her faith is rightly placed in Jesus, the Messiah. She is acting on a small nugget of truth planted in her mind and heart years earlier as she listened to the oral law. She is willing to risk public humiliation to act on what she believes.

Not only does Jesus commend her faith, but He also publicly affirms her healing. If she had left unnoticed, the stigma of bleeding would have lingered. Jesus, however, is telling every onlooker that the once bleeding woman who was considered ceremonially unclean, is indeed healed and, therefore clean. Don't miss this! Through His simple words, Jesus publicly restores her to the Jewish community. There is no longer any need or excuse to avoid her. The barrier to fellowship with others has been removed.

Jesus also tells her to *go in peace.* Because peace only comes from God, Jesus is reassuring her that she is at peace with God. He is also telling her that God's peace is with her. Jesus not only heals her physically but also heals her spiritually. The Law has been fulfilled in Christ. She is ceremonially clean. There is no longer any barrier to her public worship. The greater reality is that Jesus gives her new life in Him. Though in the moment she does not fully understand it all, the woman has been given a relationship with God like she has never known before. She will also have a community of believers who follow Christ.

The once pitiful woman who picked her way through an unsuspecting crowd is now healed, redeemed, and restored. Christ does more than she dared to hope for. He brings her out of the shadows and into His glorious light. Jesus changes everything.

The Importance of Community

The woman in Luke 8 suffered from an illness, but she also suffered from isolation. She had no interaction with people, no fellowship with others, no community. I have five millennial children. *Community* is a word they use often. While most people, including my five children, value good community, their criteria and expectations differ. In general, community can be defined as people connected to one another through a shared purpose and a shared relationship.

Every person seeks community in some form because God made us that way. People might seek community with others through a variety of shared purposes and relationships. Clubs, organizations, neighborhoods, family, and close friends can satisfy, to a degree, the need for community. However, God's perfect criteria for community is that the shared purpose and shared relationship center on Him.

From the beginning, God designed people to need other people. When He created Adam, Scripture says God knew it wasn't good for Adam to be alone, so God created Eve

(Genesis 2:18, 22). The family is God's introduction of community. Afterwards, all of God's eternal plans for mankind take place in the context of God's unique and wonderful community. In the Old Testament, God's community is Israel. In the New Testament, it is the church.

God's plan for redemption has always been in place even before creation, but we see it begin to unfold in the Old Testament through the nation of Israel. God chose Abraham to be the father of a nation that would bless the world (Genesis 12:2-3). Abraham's grandson Jacob, whose name is later changed to Israel, has twelve sons. The twelve tribes of the nation of Israel originate through Jacob's sons. Throughout Scripture, God deals with the nation of Israel as a unique community. The criteria of community is their relationship with God—a people bound to God because He loved them and chose them (Deuteronomy 7:6-8). Their shared purpose is to be a holy nation, serving as God's priests to the world (Exodus 19:6).

The Old Testament is sometimes baffling to us because we don't often think in terms of the community as a whole. Even though we need community, we think and operate primarily as individuals. While God loves the individual and deals with individual people regularly in the Old Testament, He primarily deals with Israel as a whole. Certainly, His eternal plan for redemption involves individuals. However,most of the stories we read about individuals in the Old Testament must be understood within the context of the nation of Israel. Israel, as one entity, is the focus of God's work in the Old Testament.

Early on, God tells Israel that their obedience to Him as a nation will have a positive effect on the whole nation. Consequently, overall neglect and disobedience will have an adverse effect on the whole nation (Deuteronomy 7:9-11). Even more sobering, individual sin as well as individual obedience also effects the whole nation. When we read the Old Testament with modern eyes we can be tempted to question God's motives and actions as He deals with His people. At times, we may be tempted to think, "That's not fair!" One story immediately comes to my mind.

After Moses dies, Joshua leads the nation of Israel into Canaan. The goal is to possess the land God has given them. Their first battle is a jaw-dropping victory. All of the people participate in some way (Joshua 6:5). The walls of Jericho fall and Israel captures the city. However, God's command before the battle is specific. No one is to take any spoils of war for themselves. Everything in the captured city belongs to God (Joshua 6: 17-18). The command is for *all* the people. The consequences for disobedience will affect *all* the people of Israel. One man ruined it for everyone.

An Israelite man named Achan thinks he can steal a few items from Jericho and no one will notice. But God notices, and His anger burns against the entire nation (Joshua 7:1). In fact, in their second battle, Israel is soundly defeated and thirty-six Israelite men are killed by the enemy. All of the people of Israel are shaken and affected by the stunning defeat. Joshua is left scratching his head wondering what went wrong. God's response to Joshua's bewilderment is direct and inclusive of *all* the people.

So the Lord said to Joshua, "Rise up! Why is it that you have fallen on your face? Israel has sinned and they have transgressed my covenant which I commanded them. And they have taken some of the things under the ban, and have both stolen and deceived. Moreover, they have also put them among their own things. Therefore the sons of Israel cannot stand before their enemies...(Joshua 7:1-12a).

Wait a minute. All of Israel did not sin. Achan sinned. So what is God telling us about Himself in this story? God is vividly reminding the entire nation of Israel that all sin is serious, even individual sin. He is also reminding them that all sin has serious consequences, not only for the individual sinner but also for the nation as a whole. God deals with His people as a community. Sin threatens their collective fellowship with God and their collective purpose of glorifying God.

Joshua follows God's instructions for dealing with sin. *The entire nation* is told to consecrate themselves, which includes bathing to get physically clean and then putting on clean clothes. Consecration is a physical action that illustrates a spiritual condition. Afterwards, Joshua is given instructions to find the individual who actually sinned. Achan is discovered and confesses. The stolen items are found hidden in his tent. His entire family has been aware and even complicit with the sin and the coverup of sin. God tells Joshua to burn everything Achan owns, and then the people of Israel are to kill Achan and all of his family (Joshua 7:16-26).

Harsh is an understatement! Before you feel sorry for poor old Achan, let the gravity of the story sink in. Sin is serious and affects everything and everyone! God will go to great lengths to root out sin in His community because the wildfire effect of sin will eventually engulf everyone.

After Israel deals with Achan's sin according to God's instructions, God blesses Israel with a great victory over the very city that defeated them. With mercy and grace, God uses

Israel's past failure to secure the victory. The blessings of obedience flow to the entire nation of Israel (Joshua 8).

Throughout the Old Testament the importance of community and the corporate impact of disobedience and obedience to God is reiterated over and over. Community is God's design—people connected to one another in shared relationship to God and shared purpose for God. Everything an individual does within God's community has some degree of impact on the whole. To God, community is sacred.

God doesn't change. He is the same God in the New Testament as He is in the Old Testament. God's eternal plans continue to unfold through a community of people. In the New Testament, God's community is the church. It still is.

The Apostle Paul compares the church to the human body. The human body is one body but has many parts, or members. His analogy explains that when one part of the physical body hurts, every part hurts. Likewise, one body part is not more important than another. The foot is not more important than the hand. The ear is not more important than the eye. All the parts of the human body are useful and valued.

Paul teaches us that the church functions like a physical body, one body with many members. Like the human body, every member of the church has purpose and is valued. Likewise, when one member suffers, all the members suffer. When one member is honored, all the members are honored. The church, as the body of Christ, functions both individually and corporately for God's purpose (1 Corinthians 12: 12-26).

The power source for the church is the Holy Spirit. He indwells each individual believer, and He also binds individual Christians together as one community in Christ (Ephesians 2:2-10, 3:3-6). He blesses individual believers with spiritual gifts at the moment of salvation. Spiritual gifts are to be used for building up the entire body of Christ (Ephesians 311-12).

While Scripture gives us a very clear picture of the church as one body with many members, today's Christian almost always defaults to the rights and privileges of the individual. We tend to think our relationship with Christ, as well as our lifestyle, is a personal matter with little or no bearing on others. God, however, insists the community, the church, is a collective unit whereby each individual person affects the whole. Individual sin as well as individual obedience has communal impact. Furthermore, meaningful connection to the community is vital if the individual Christian is going to mature and flourish.

The world is filled with people who need Jesus and the community God offers in Christ. While the church is God's rich blessing to every believer it is also the hands and feet of Christ operating in the world. If the collective church makes an impact on the world and other believers, it is because individual Christians are surrendered to Christ, living to glorify Him.

As believers in Christ, how do we strengthen, enhance, and guard God's community? What is our individual responsibility within the community? How do we reach out to those who need God's community? How do we give as well as receive from other believers? How can the church, the community of God's people, live and work as a healthy collective organism in a sinful world?

The New Testament is filled with teaching, instruction, and admonition concerning Christian living within the context of God's community. We will briefly discuss four general principles that will help strengthen our personal connection to the community as well as help the entire community glorify God. As you continue to read, remember…everything we do or don't do as individual followers of Christ has communal impact.

Love One Another

It sounds simple, but it isn't. People are the great sandpaper of life, always rubbing us the wrong way. Even within the church, personalities clash, opinions differ, and preferences easily take precedence. Still, the Bible says *love one another*. Loving other people is not an empty platitude we toss around at church. It is an action, an outward demonstration to others of the sacrificial love we have received from God through Christ.

During the last Passover meal that Jesus shares with His disciples, He gives them a powerful example of love in action. After the meal, Jesus removes His outer garment. Wearing only the tunic style undergarment, the garment of a servant or slave, He wraps a towel around His waist and pours water into a basin. To their dismay, the Messiah, the King of Glory, God Incarnate stoops to wash the road dust from His prideful, arguing, imperfect disciples' feet, even the feet of Judas (John13:1-20, Luke 22:14-24). Jesus' powerful example of service is soon followed by a command.

A new commandment I give to you, that you love one another, even as I have loved you, that you also love one another. By this all men will know that you are My disciples, if you have love for one another. (John 13:34-35)

For the disciples, the commandment to love one another is not a new commandment. They knew plenty of verses from the

Old Testament about loving God and loving others. While the command to love one another is not new, the disciples have just witnessed a new example of love. Through Jesus' willingness to wash their feet, they gain a fresh perspective about loving others.

The disciples misunderstood so many things. They argued over who would be the greatest and who would sit at Jesus' right hand and at His left hand when He became King. They associate being served, being loved, and being important with following Jesus. That night in the Upper Room, Jesus turns their thinking upside down—again. Love, not power and position, is the hallmark of an individual Christian. Love is also the distinguishing characteristic of God's community, the church.

For many Christians, community can be disrupted by various things. Pain, sorrow, sin, pride, doubt, hurt, and unforgiveness are a few of the things that can damage and deter fellowship with other believers. Love is the blanket we wrap around a wounded believer, no matter how or why those wounds were inflicted. The love Jesus requires of us looks and acts like His love. It is not sappy sentiment nor is it universal tolerance. It is truthful yet full of mercy, direct yet overflowing with compassion. Agape love is an act of will—loving people as they need to be loved. As we learn to love one another within the church, we gain a powerful platform to share the Good News of Christ with unbelievers.

My friend Amy recently lost her husband John. The loss came after John's unexpected brain stroke, an extended hospital stay, and finally hospice care. John was only fifty-seven when he died. He and Amy still had one child living at home. John and Amy occasionally attended a local church, but their son was an active participant in the student ministry of that church.

Throughout the months of John's hospitalization, the church Amy and John had been attending, reached out with comfort and encouragement. The church demonstrated great love toward Amy and her grieving family. They loved her while John remained hospitalized, and they loved her as the inevitable end drew near. Her son Matthew leaned into friends within the student ministry and the leadership wrapped him in love as he faced the imminent loss of his dad. When John stepped into eternity and met Jesus face to face, the church remained steadfast in their ministry to Amy and her family. They helped her organize a meaningful celebration of life for John. Afterwards, the church, God's community of believers, continued to love her and help her through the difficult transition that lay ahead.

Amy recently wrote, "Truly, I cannot put into words how much their ministry blessed all of us. They provided exactly what we needed in the midst of our heartbreak and sadness. From this difficult experience, I gained a church family, friendships, and a place to serve. What a blessing they are to me."

Love one another. It makes a difference.

Encourage and Build Up One Another

Paul writes in Ephesians that we are to walk in love (Ephesians 5:1-2). Everything we do as Christians falls under the heading of *love one another*. It's interesting that many verses of Scripture are *one another* verses, teaching us to practically demonstrate God's love to others. Paul reminds the church that a practical application of love is to *encourage one another and build up one another, just as you are already doing* (1 Thessalonians 5:11).

To encourage means to call to one's side, to comfort, to exhort, or to advocate for someone. Encouragement is not flattery. It is speaking truth in love, strengthening another person spiritually. Paul writes about comfort that builds a person's faith—a comfort we can give to others because God's Spirit has comforted or encouraged us.

...God is our merciful Father and the source of all comfort. He comforts us in all our troubles so that we can comfort others. When they are troubled, we will be able to give them the same comfort God has given us. (2 Corinthians 1:3-4 NLT)

Encouragement can be a well-spoken or comforting word that builds another person's faith. Encouragement can also be an act of service, accompanied by no words at all. Over the years I have experienced "Jesus with shoes on"—Christians who have encouraged me through acts of kindness and service.

The day after my first husband died, two precious ladies showed up to clean my house. They knew a stream of people would be in and out of my house for several days. They also knew I would have no time to clean. Honestly, I was horrified when they showed up. As a busy wife and mom, the house was a wreck, and I was embarrassed. Those two ladies were not put off by my hesitation. With no fanfare and few words, they cleaned my house from top to bottom. I remember feeling relieved and blessed. Their kind service encouraged me, and I have never forgotten it.

The Book of Philippians admonishes us to serve with the same attitude that Christ had. He became a bondservant, serving with humility and selflessness (Philippians 2: 3-8). Listen! Jesus was no doormat for people to walk all over.

In Scripture, to be a bondservant is to be in a permanent relationship of servitude, the servant's desires are abandoned to the desires of the master. Jesus is never a bondservant of people. He serves God's purpose, doing the Father's will by serving people.

Sometimes we are afraid to invest too deeply in people for fear of being taken advantage of. As loving encouragers, we serve with God's wisdom and discernment, not bleeding hearts that can be easily manipulated or taken advantage of. The Holy Spirit directs our steps even as we serve others. Also, serving alongside other believers guards us from possible missteps and keeps us accountable as well. Lone Ranger serving can be exhausting and even hazardous to our own walk with Christ.

Pray for One Another

Prayer is simply talking to God. It is not complicated nor is it reserved for a select few. Every believer in Christ has access to God's throne of grace. The writer of Hebrews says, *Let us draw near with confidence to the throne of grace, that we may receive mercy and may find grace to help in time of need* (Hebrews 4:16). We can bring our worship, our thanks, our concerns, and our requests to the Lord at any time. When we pray, coming boldly to the throne of grace, we are exercising an intimate privilege given only to God's children. When we intercede for others, we are bearing their burdens, taking them to the source of mercy, grace, and help.

Within our community of other believers, we are often doers, busy serving and caring for other people. Prayer is sometimes overlooked because we would rather do something tangible and measurable. Prayer, however, is the greatest work we can do on behalf of others. Praying for others is a gift and a blessing to them. It is also a demonstration of love.

We know from Paul's writings that he constantly prayed for the churches he loved. Ephesians, Philippians, Colossians, and 2 Thessalonians all contain Paul's prayers for the church. These are not superficial prayers, rather they are long-term requests made to God. Paul prays for spiritual maturity, spiritual strength and wisdom, and spiritual fruit. He prays for love to flourish and for knowledge and discernment to increase. He prays that God would be glorified in the church.

His example encourages us to pray for each other with a long-term mindset. Sometimes we are so focused on the urgent needs of today, we forget that God is doing a lifelong work of conforming us to Christ (Philippians 1:6). Paul's example also reminds us to pray for the church as a whole. This includes the community of people we worship with on a regular basis and are most connected to. It also includes praying for the church worldwide.

If the Lord is pressing you to pray for someone with consistency, perhaps for years, use Pauls' prayers as you pray. Praying Scripture will keep us mindful of the big picture of God's work in their lives. Incorporating Scripture into our prayers also keeps our prayers fresh as we pray consistently for the same people. Since I pray for my family every day, I often use Colossians 1:9-12 in my prayers for them. I have my children's names written beside these verses in my Bible, reminding me to pray for spiritual blessings and spiritual maturity in my children.

Praying for others involves long-term, big-picture praying, but as the body of Christ, we also pray for one another's daily needs. Certainly God is interested in everything about us.

He cares about the smallest details of our lives. When Jesus
teaches His disciples to pray, He teaches them to ask for daily
bread (Matthew 6:9-13). Bread, food for the day, is an ongoing
need. Jesus is encouraging us to pray for daily, ongoing needs.
For people who have everything at their fingertips, praying for
the smallest of daily needs seems frivolous. For most of the
world, everyday needs are a huge concern.

Jesus tells us not to be anxious about what we eat or what
clothes we will wear, but that doesn't mean stop praying about
those things (Matthew 6:31-32). Replacing worry with trust
in His provision starts with confident praying—taking daily
needs, yes every need, to the throne of grace.

*Be anxious for nothing, but in everything by prayer and
supplication with thanksgiving, let your requests be made
known to God. And the peace of God, which surpasses all
comprehension, shall guard your hearts and your minds in
Christ Jesus.* (Philippians 4:6-7)

Daily needs are a primary source of stress in much of the
world, even for Christians. As we pray with and for one another
about everyday needs, Scripture reminds us how to pray.

There are three words in Philippians 4:6 that give direction
to our prayers: *prayer, supplication, and thanksgiving.* In the
original language, the word for *prayer* used in this verse is a
general word for prayer, but it has the connotation of worship.
When we come to God in prayer, we come with a humble
worshipping heart. Worship puts every request into perspective
reminding us that nothing is too great for Him; neither is any
detail too small for Him to notice. We bring our requests to
God, our *supplications* with an attitude of worship. Making a

request is not a demand, neither is it claiming something God has not already promised in His Word. Our requests, however, should be specific and energetic. Asking specifically is for our benefit, giving us an opportunity to look back and see how God has answered or provided.

The third word is *thanksgiving*. Interestingly, Scripture is teaching us to be thankful before the request is answered. When we are thankful before we see the results of our prayers, we are cultivating an attitude of thankfulness that has nothing to do with requests but has everything to do with God Himself. We learn to be thankful however He chooses to answer our requests, even if He says no or takes our requests in a completely different direction. Being thankful before we see results requires faith, trusting God to supply all of our needs in His time and in His way.

When we pray with a worshipping heart, bringing specific requests with thanksgiving, God's peace steps in. Like a guard at his post, God's peace guards our thoughts and feelings. When we pray, the Lord ushers in a peace we will never fully understand. The watching world will never understand either, but they will notice. People around us will eventually become aware that a praying Christian consistently lives in peace.

As we pray for God to meet the daily needs of those around us, let me be quick to add that often God uses us, the church individually and collectively, to meet those needs. James reminds us that faith with no works is a dead faith (James 2:14-16). We can pray all day, but if God tells us to give food to the hungry or put gas in someone's car or repair their roof or give them a coat—seek God's wisdom and then get up and obey! Loving one another, encouraging one another, and praying for one another are all tied together. While prayer is our first response to any kind of need people may have, love and encouragement in action are often the hands and feet of Jesus, putting a human face to God's reply.

We have discussed praying long-term prayers for others and praying for daily needs, but the things that most often compel us to run to the throne of grace are urgent needs. We pray more often and more tenaciously when circumstances are dire, when children are suffering, when friends are sick, when failure looms or when relationships crumble.

One of life's greatest blessings is praying friends. When my burden is too great to carry alone, I share it with another Christian woman I trust will pray. The Gospel of Mark gives us a riveting account of friends bringing another friend to Jesus. While the story is not specially about prayer, we can correctly apply the truth of the passage to prayer.

Jesus has returned to Capernaum. His popularity increases every time He enters the city. News spreads quickly that He is back home and staying in a house, probably with friends. Jesus does what He always does wherever He goes—He teaches. On this day, His teaching may have started as a casual conversation with His hosts, but people begin showing up at the door. The house soon fills up with listeners. The windows are open so the overflow crowd leans in to hear Him. Even the local religious leaders poke their heads in to hear, eager to scrutinize anything Jesus says. The crowd is in no hurry to leave and is probably growing by the minute, blocking any entry through the doors or windows of the house.

A group of friends round the corner, rushing toward the house where they have been told Jesus is staying. They are breathing hard when they arrive. The friends have physically carried another friend to see Jesus. The friend is a paralytic man, unable to walk, lying on a mat, wondering what an encounter with Jesus will hold. When the group of friends see the pressing crowd and realize the impossibility of getting to Jesus, tenacity and ingenuity take over. They decide to go through the roof.

I'm not sure which friend came up with the idea. Maybe it took him a few minutes to persuade the others. Their love and concern for the paralytic friend overrides any concern for safety, embarrassment, or repair bills. They somehow, haul their immobile friend to the roof, carefully lay the man down on his mat, and begin to dig a hole in the roof right above Jesus.

Surely falling debris stops everything going on in the house. All eyes look upward. When the hole is big enough, those tenacious, loving friends gently lower the paralytic man, still on his mat, until he safely rests in front of Jesus. The Bible says, *Seeing their faith, Jesus said to the paralyzed man, "My child, your sins are forgiven"* (Mark 2:5 NLT).

Did you catch that? Jesus sees the *faith of the friends* that brought the man. Jesus doesn't mention the faith of the paralyzed man. Those guys don't just love their paralyzed friend; they trust Jesus so much they are willing to haul a grown man across town, carry him to a roof, tear the roof off, and lower the man down. They have labored while exercising great faith. Jesus commends their faith and heals their friend both spiritually and physically (Mark 2:5-12).

There are so many things to draw from this story. However, I want to apply this account to prayer. Notice again the great need of the paralytic man resigned to live on a homemade palette or mat. Also notice the tenacity and the faith of his friends. Praying for the overwhelming needs of others is like carrying someone's mat to Jesus. When the need is great, we pray for others with unashamed tenacity and faith wrapped in great love.

When we pray for urgent needs, we still pray as we are instructed in Philippians 4. We pray with a worshiping attitude, knowing God is on HIs throne and nothing is impossible or too great for Him. We present our urgent request specifically, not claiming the outcome, but lifting that need to the throne of grace with confident faith. Faith does not demand that God responds according to our plans or our desired outcome. Praying in faith requires that we hold every urgent request with open, thankful hands—surrendered to our holy and loving Lord, no matter how or when He answers.

Volumes have been written about prayer. This short section of one chapter in one book does not begin to scratch the surface of the magnificent blessing of prayer. My purpose is to admonish us to pray for others, especially those in our community of believers. Pray for God's long-term work in people's lives. Pray for their daily needs. Pray for the urgent needs that arise with complete trust in God. Praying for one another is essential to God's community of believers. Prayer has lasting impact on the life of individuals as well as the entire community.

Forgive One Another

Loving one another, encouraging one another, and praying for one another may seem simple compared to forgiving one another. Many people walk away from churches and Christians in general because of wounds they have incurred from other Christians.

I get it. I grew up as a pastor's daughter. I married a pastor. When he died, I married another pastor. I have lived my entire life connected to a community of believers, not only through a relationship with Christ but also through my dad's, my husbands', and my vocation. Through the years, people in the church have hurt me and my family. I could tell you things that people have said and done that would curl your toenails—some things so horrific...I will never forget them. The Lord never promises we will forget the wrongs done to us, but He does tell us to forgive.

And be kind to one another, tender-hearted, forgiving each other, just as God in Christ also has forgiven you. (Ephesians 4:32)

How do we forgive deep hurts and wrongs done to us? First, we remember that we have been forgiven. We came into this world as sinners, corrupted through and through, hopeless, spiritually dead, and separated from God. But God steps in to our hopeless condition and extends grace. We are forgiven, cleansed, and made new by His grace (Ephesians 2:1-5, 8-9). We also need to remember that as Christians we are still capable of sinning. Because of Jesus Christ, we have ongoing forgiveness available to us. Daily confessing our sin, even confessing our propensity to sin, and asking for daily cleansing keeps us tuned in, ever mindful that we are a holy people set apart for God's glory (1 John 1:9, 1 Peter 1:14-19).

Forgiveness is a release. We release our hurt to God, trusting Him to heal our wounds and even use our wounds to bring honor to Him. We also release to God the person who offended or hurt us, trusting God to deal with that person however He chooses. Within the church, Jesus gives us instructions for dealing with repeat offenders who claim to be Christians (Matthew 18:15-17). We are to be wise and discerning in our dealings with all people, especially other believers. We are to forgive freely, trusting God every step of the way. Keep in mind, however, what forgiveness is not.

- Forgiveness is not denial of the pain. It is acknowledging the pain and releasing it to God.
- Forgiveness does not necessarily erase the consequences of someone's actions.
- Forgiveness does not guarantee restored trust or a renewed relationship with the one who hurt you.
- Forgiveness is not a one-time event. Deep wounds can resurface in our lives. When they do, we must forgive again. This does not mean we rehash old events with the offender. It means we continue to release both the deep wound and the offender to God.
- Forgiveness does not wait to be asked. Offenders may not know or care they have wounded us. They may have already died. It may be unwise to reach back and stir up toxic relationships. Forgiveness can be between you and the Lord. Forgiveness is most importantly about our relationship to Christ.

Also keep in mind, there will be times when *we need to receive forgiveness* from a fellow believer in Christ. When we are the offender, whether intentional or not, we can humble ourselves and ask forgiveness not only from the person we have wounded but also from the Lord. If a person forgives, receive it with humility and gratitude. If the offended person is unwilling to forgive, give time and space for prayer and for God to mend and change unwilling hearts. If divisions arise because of unforgiveness, seek godly counsel. Unforgiveness can quickly become a trap and a spiritual stumbling block for any of us.

Conclusion

Community is important. God has designed us for community. As followers of Christ, we are bound to other Christians by our shared relationship with Christ and our shared purpose in Christ. We need each other. Loving, encouraging, praying, and forgiving one another—these actions all strengthen our faith, build up the church, expand God's kingdom, and give us a powerful testimony for a world searching for community. Dear one, we cannot live the Christian life isolated from other believers. If we try, we will live a half-life, far beneath God's design for brothers and sisters in Christ.

There are not enough pages in this book to tell you all the wonderful blessings I have received through other Christians. Every moment of my life believers in Christ has loved me through awkward stages, painful events, and great joys. I have been encouraged and my faith strengthened countless times by another Christian's sensitivity and truthfulness. I have been prayed for often and for every reason imaginable. I have tearfully and joyfully expericend forgiveness from people I have wounded, and I have released and forgiven the ones who have wounded me. The blessings of living in fellowship with God's people far outweigh the disappointments and hurts that always come when people ae involved. We need each other. We need God's community of believers.

I love the woman in Luke 8. I love that she set her face toward Jesus and Jesus responded with both healing and restoration. I hope heaven has a replay button so we can see the rest of her story someday. Can you imagine her first hug in twelve years or her pain-free laughter with friends and family or her first worship experience with fellow believers? Her isolated life is replaced with the beauty of community. Jesus changes everything. He did for her. He will for you.

As I write the closing words of this book, I am so thankful that God sees us even while we live on the edge of desperate. He meets us on the dusty plains of desperation, always working on our behalf and for His glory. His ways and His plans may differ from ours, but we can trust Him. He is doing a new and good work in us. *Will you see it? He is making a roadway in the wilderness and rivers in the desert.*

Discussion Questions
Desperate for Community

1. The woman in Luke 8 is both sick and isolated. In your opinion, which is worse? For the woman, how does Jesus deal with both issues? What does her story reveal to us about God?

2. The woman wanted to be healed and then quietly slip away. Why does Jesus prevent this? What greater purpose does He have for her life?

3. God designed all of us with a need for community. What is a general definition for community? How can we define God's community? How has God's community of people impacted your life?

4. In the Old Testament, the New Testament, and even now, God deals with His community collectively and individually. Everything an individual believer does or doesn't do has a communal effect. Talk about this. Why is communal effect such a difficult concept for many Christians today? Does Paul's analogy in 1 Corinthians 12:12-27 help clarify the collective and individual aspect of the church, God's community?

5. Jesus demonstrates love in action when He washes His disciples feet (John 13: 5). Afterwards, He tells them to love one another (John 13:34). Have you ever been the recipient of love in action from a believer in Christ?

6. Read 1 Thessalonians 5:11. How can we practically live out this verse? Within the context of God's community, can you give a personal example of encouraging someone or being encouraged by someone?

7. Praying for one another is a wonderful privilege. Read Philippians 4:6-7. Discuss the importance of worship, supplication, and thanksgiving as they pertain to prayer.

8. What is forgiveness? What is forgiveness not? Read Ephesians 4:32. If we know Christ, we have experienced His forgiveness. Why is it important to forgive others, especially other believers in Christ?

9. Is there someone you know who is sick and isolated— someone who needs God's community of people? How can you be the hands and feet of Jesus to this person?

Resources

Do You Believe, Paul David Tripp

Dark Clouds, Deep Mercy, Mark Vroegop

Experiencing God, Henry Blackaby

facinglossblog.com D. Ray Davis

Hind's Feet on High Places, Hannah Hurnard

Hope Heals, Jay and Katherine Wolf

Life Without Lack, Dallas Willard

The Ever-Loving Truth, Voddie Baucham

The Prodigal God, Timothy Keller

The Purpose Driven Life, Rick Warren

The Transforming Power of the Gospel, Jerry Bridges

Treasures in the Dark, Katherine Wolf

Trusting God, Jerry Bridges

Suffering is Never for Nothing, Elizabeth Elliot

When God Doesn't Fix It, Laura Story

When God is Silent, Charles Swindoll

Thank You

A project like this book is never a one person show. It takes a team of people using their unique skills and gifts to bring a book into existence. My heart is overflowing with gratitude as I write this page.

Thank you *Karen Murphree* for the hours and hours you spent proofreading, correcting, suggesting edits, and encouraging me along the way. I could not have done this project without you. You are a godsend and a blessing to me.

Thank you to the team of people who have each crafted with excellence a specialized part of this book:

Juanita Jones, thank you for formulating intuitive discussion questions. Your insightful expertise in leading small group discussion is amazing! I am so thankful God has blessed me with your friendship.

Micah Mathewson, thank you for designing the perfect cover to convey the message of this book. I love you, son. You bless me always.

Lee Ann Martin, thank you for the layout design, the prayers, the encouragement, and the rich friendship spanning more than forty years.

Tonya Price, thank you sweet friend for always taking great photos. Thanks for laughing with me about my insecurities and at the same time accommodating for them.

Tim Passmore, thank you for creating an outlet for writers through **Outcome Publishing**. You are meeting a need and providing an avenue for many people to hear the gospel.

Thank you to the women of Venice Florida who attend the annual Winter Bible Study. This book came out of our 2023 study together. You are the ones who pressed me to continue writing. Thank you for your encouragement and prayers throughout the process. Thank you for showing up every January and February for the past eleven years. God has done a good work among us.

Thank you to the three churches who have graciously hosted the Word of Joy Winter Bible Study for years. *First Baptist Church Venice, Venice Presbyterian Church, and Grace Community Bible Church,* thank you for being lights for Christ in Southwest Florida. Thank you for investing in hundreds of women through Winter Bible Study, welcoming us each year with open arms.

Thank you *Pastor Eric Hernandez* for working alongside me to provide a Spanish translation of this book. Through your work, I believe many Spanish readers will be strengthened in their faith, and many others will meet Christ for the first time. You are a blessing to me, just as you are to so many others.

Thank you to the *Word of Joy* team. Whew! Who knew God would accomplish so much through a small group of women? You were willing to take on the challenge of ministering to women eight years ago. We have watched God do miracles here at home as well as internationally. *Betty Jo Faulkner. Lois Ann Murphree, Tonya Price, Molly Graybill, Brenda Bartlett, Honey Ziegler, Amy Schriber, and Kate Burda,* you have all served in timely and unique capacities. Thank you, thank you, thank you! Also, thank you to every volunteer, prayer warrior, encourager, and generous contributor. You are the golden threads in the Word of Joy tapestry.

Thank you to *my family.* You are a great joy and blessing to me. You have prayed for me, encouraged me, and cheered for me all along the way—not only in writing this book, but also in life. I love you all.

Thank you to my husband, *Allen.* What a journey life has been! What a journey writing this book has been!. Thank you for patiently eating off of paper plates and a TV tray while the kitchen table remained strewn with papers, books, Bibles ,and a computer. You never complained—you just encouraged me to keep going. I love you.

Thank you, *Heavenly Father* for Your enduring love and Your kind patience toward me. Thank you for giving me a season to write. Indeed, You make a roadway in the wilderness and rivers in the desert.

www.ingramcontent.com/pod-product-compliance
Lightning Source LLC
LaVergne TN
LVHW091718130225
803680LV00030B/348

* 9 780996 964586 *